296.3
W83   Wolf, Arnold Jacob, comp.
           What is man?

296.3
W83   Wolf, Arnold Jacob, comp.
           What is man?

Temple Israel Library
Minneapolis, Minn.

Please sign your full name on the above card.

Return books promptly to the Library or Temple Office.

Fines will be charged for overdue books or for damage or loss of same.

WHAT IS MAN?

Jewish Sources Speak Books
Eugene B. Borowitz, Editor

WHAT IS MAN?, Arnold J. Wolf
A SENSE OF DUTY, Simcha Kling

WHAT IS MAN?

Rabbi Arnold J. Wolf

A B'NAI B'RITH BOOK

The B'nai B'rith Department of Adult Jewish Education, organized in 1954, has as its purpose to stimulate and promote the study of Judaism among adult Jews. Through annual Institutes of Judaism, year-round discussion groups, and authoritative and readable publications, it helps individuals and groups plan study programs on the religious and cultural heritage of the Jewish people.

To my wife who,
by being so complete a woman,
has shown me what it might be to become a man.

FOREWORD

Each volume of *The Jewish Sources Speak* books is designed to give the modern reader insight into a major theme of Judaism as expressed in its classic texts, particularly the post-Biblical. The readings have been selected with two basic criteria in mind: their relevance to the general concept around which each book centers and their representativeness of their Jewish literary genre. Only selections which treat at some length of the specific idea involved are utilized so as to afford the reader an in-depth exposure to each particular style of Jewish expression.

In the interests of clarity and readability, a few liberties have been permitted in the rendering of the passages. In certain instances, for example, repetitious material has been deleted. Almost all the texts are freely paraphrased rather than translated literally. Countering the loss of specific literary styles is, hopefully, a gain in the more central goal of communicating direct understanding of the ideas and thought processes involved. The texts are printed almost entirely without notes or the kind of commentary which usually accompanies them to clarify their intent. Instead, the commentary is incorporated into the texts themselves.

To further facilitate understanding of the way in which the various literary forms and intellectual patterns have contributed to an integrated Jewish life style, the selections are not arranged chronologically in order of composition but appear in terms of their thematic concerns. Where existing translations have been reprinted appropriate acknowledgments are made. Otherwise renderings are by the author of the specific volume.

This approach to Jewish ideas via the classic texts of Judaism makes it possible to present only the most significant aspects of each concept. There is intentionally no concluding or summary chapter. It is hoped that the thoughtful reader, introduced in this way to some of the Jewish classics, will be encouraged to go on to available translations of the full works. Thus familiarized with an important and relevant area of Jewish belief and of the varied Jewish literature in which it has been expressed and developed, he will be better equipped to tackle the Jewish sources themselves.

For critical reading of the manuscript and for numerous helpful suggestions, I am indebted to Dr. Norman E. Frimer, Rabbi Oscar Groner, Dr. Louis L. Kaplan and Mr. Earl Morse. For general editing and for preparing the manuscript for press, my thanks go to Mrs. Lily Edelman, Director of B'nai B'rith's Commission on Adult Jewish Education; and for seeing the book through the press, to Miss Naomi Thompson, the Commission's Director of Production and Promotion.

Finally, a warm word of appreciation goes to Professor Oscar I. Janowsky, former Chairman of the Publications Committee of the Commission, under whose leadership this project was originally conceived and approved.

Night by Elie Wiesel is from the author's novel of the same name, © Les Editions de Minuit, 1958. English translation © MacGibbon & Kee. Reprinted by permission of Hill and Wang, Inc.

Eugene B. Borowitz,
General Editor

INTRODUCTION

Man is a mystery. What he is admits no single solution or scientific answer. He is the very question he is asking, the riddle he would unravel. Man's nature is wondrous, complex, infinitely mysterious. He images God, the Supreme Mystery.

Accordingly, our investigation of Jewish sources presented here can only open up the question of what man is. Our only goal is by the very probing to make that question more vivid. Hopefully, our study will make us less dogmatic about our own character and more eager to respond to the mystery of man as it is manifest in our own lives.

For man is concerned with nothing more deeply than he is with man. The biological sciences lead us with growing momentum from protoplasm to the human being. The social sciences are all about man: his mind, his history, his family, his life, his communities, his mysterious self. The great religions of the East are wholly centered in man: God is either man's therapist or his Savior, if there is any God at all. In Christianity one Man is deemed fit to be a Divine Person. In Judaism, man is taught to master the world and finally to meet the Master of all worlds.

The dignity and centrality of man are essential Jewish teachings. Why was man created last in the order of creation, our Rabbis ask. One answer is evolutionary: man is the summit of creation, the honored guest who enters the house of feasting only after all others have made their preparations. But the other view deflates our self-centeredness: man came last so that even an insect could say, "My father was here before your father." In the order of creation man is a latecomer, an interloper, an epiphenomenon.

Judaism's view of man is dialectical. It asserts emphatically the worth of man, but it knows that despite his pretensions he is not God. Judaism believes that man is "good," but not so good as he thinks, nor is he only good. Judaism is a religion for men, not disembodied spirits, freaks, or saints, but it asks real men to be more than they are or would like to be. Judaism promises man eternity, but it knows he must die; his eternity is not inherent in his humanity but is rather a transmutation of that humanity. Judaism is patient with man, but insistent that he grow; the God of Judaism is in love with man, yet His love is anything but blind. Nor is Judaism blind to the pretensions, the phoniness, the hollowness of man. Despite all that Judaism knows man permits himself to be, however, he is still the image of God, the only symbol and the only proof of God, the friend of God, His partner in dialogue, His son.

In our own time, we have lost both poles of this traditional Jewish dialectic. Where once man seemed noble and profound, he now appears impotent, doomed. The proud master of creation who was to subdue the beasts and the fish and the birds has, indeed, conquered the ocean's depths and the sky's secret spaces, but he feels neither confident nor safe. Never was man so rich and so anxious, so powerful and so empty. Modern man has accomplished much; but he is afraid no Father cares, and so his triumph is dust in his mouth. He may do much, have much, learn much, achieve much, but he finds it hard to believe that he is much. Being, not having, is what finally counts; we are affluent of goods but poor of self.

Perhaps that is why man is so often dehumanized in his actions toward other men. In the secret Nazi jargon the language of murder was that of pest exterminators: men were insects, the world could be made "clean" of Jews. Auschwitz was not a place where real men were killed; it was a crematory for vermin and lice. Nor was it the Jew alone who was not permitted to be a man; enough gas remained on VE Day to kill twice as many persons as had already been exterminated. If Jews were less than human, Poles, Slavs, Gypsies and millions of Aryans were no longer men either. The doctrine of racial superiority masked a deeper, darker philosophy: that evolution can be reversed, that given the proper effort and technique man can wholly succeed in becoming a brute. The incredible and the unimaginable nadir of human degradation became reality in a way that no new theory of man can ever ignore. In our own days, wars continue to destroy life; men watch other men getting killed across the street and do not even call the police. It is as though we observe the shooting down of dogs, the swatting of flies.

In our thought life too there has been a steady, principled dehumanization of man. The more naive biologists have tried to convince us that man is his body and that his body is not significantly different from matter as such. While some scientists writhe under terrifying new dilemmas of the chemistry of life, the layman is informed that all problems are about to be solved: man is an ingenious chemical factory, his brain a computer. In these systems, typical of nineteenth-century high-culture and twentieth-century popular opinion, man is no longer worthy of respect and concern; he is an object of curiosity, disdain, sometimes of disgust. He is anything but a person. He has intricacy but is devoid of dignity.

In contemporary imaginative literature, this theme has been worked with extraordinary persuasiveness. Particularly in the Theater of the Absurd, we have come to expect men to be portrayed as beasts, insects, psychopaths, offal. At first we may have found these depictions revolting, but over the years we have come to see them as naturalistic. In the madmen and pederasts and animals of modern literature we do, in fact, recognize ourselves. When we inquire of the mirror on the wall who is fairest of all, the answer that comes back unmistakably is: "Not you, not you, anything but you." That is how far our twentieth-century rejection of man has brought us.

We are suffering from the disease of reductionism. Biology has tried to reduce man to protoplasm, psychology sees him as made up of drives, history views him as victim, literature as absurd. And it is men who have done this to man: there has been no revealed doctrine of degradation, no Torah of the Absurd. Of his own will man has come to see himself diminished. Man has made man inhuman, so that man can act the beast. His disconnection from the Divine unhinges him from himself.

Our response to this situation is often a flight into sentimental self-defense. When it is said man is evil, we respond he has his good side, too. If man is accused of being diabolic, we say he is an angel with a dirty face. Artistic representations of him as hollow or bestial are denounced.

As for Jews, some assert that Judaism's unique message to the world is that man is "good," and history the progressive evolution of his character. They read the complex Jewish sources as blandly asserting that man is really beneficent, that his iniquities are mere mistakes. They would have us believe, against the testimony of wisdom and experience both, that human beings are basically kind, affectionate, self-sacrificing and generous. What little evil man manifests is only a heritage from his primitive past that time and education will surely and swiftly overcome. Indeed, that is what most nineteenth-century westernized Jews thought and how many still define traditional Judaism. That kind of naive liberalism makes man god, judge, creator, the only hope.

But this idolization of man is hard to support. The dehumanization of man has been a terrible self-fulfilling reality in our years of holocaust and their aftermath. We are thrown back on the realism of the Jewish estimate of man.

This estimate is documented in modern times in Sigmund Freud's subtle and decisive doctrine of man, in which Jewish categories are recovered and the Jewish dialectic brought alive. Trained as a physiologist and physician, Freud understands that man is an animal, his body an animal body, and his spirit coordinate with, if not simply another name for, his body. He refutes medieval Christianity's pretensions of man's "spirituality" and European rationalism's exaltation of human reason. He admits no either/or; man is *both* body and psyche, *both* good and evil, *both* irrational and rational, *both* sick and curable.

Freud teaches us that dangers beset the self on every side; it is hard to be human. Sanity is in permanent crisis. Selfhood is man's rarest achievement. Love and death compete for his loyalty. Man's sexuality, construed by Freud as the instinct for life and pleasure, offers man an Eden of the imagination from which the demands of reality inevitably expel him. Love leaves us conflicted.

And death, it turns out, is not only our destiny, it is also our deep human wish. Every death is a kind of suicide; no man survives his own drive to die. Therapy is, in principle at least, interminable because neurosis is indestructible. The self is a battlefield on which is fought out every primitive skirmish; the war goes on, and if it is never won, neither need it ever be wholly lost. That is what Freud said about man, and, despite his imitators and revisers, no one has known as accurately as he the nature of twentieth-century man.

But there is more to be said—and it is Martin Buber who amplifies Freud. To know oneself is, as Freud had already guessed, to be known by another. Indeed, one only becomes a self in interpersonal encounter. But this means that the id and the ego themselves are not just given; they are somehow made. The unconscious is not, Buber insists in his great book *The Knowledge of Man,* simply dredged up; it is created. The inner machinery of humanity is not fundamentally inherited. It is produced out of numberless meetings or dialogues with other men and the one great meeting with God which lies at the center of them all.

Man finally discovers himself, then, not through analysis but through inter-relationship, not by thought about thought, but by life shared with people. True wisdom requires both personal renunciation and a reaching out to family, people, the world. Health needs both self-acceptance and self-transcendence, achieved only in the life of dialogue. To come to be oneself, one must enter into relationships with others, with parents and friends, with the beloved "other." Man cannot achieve selfhood without accepting the terrible risk of living with others, an intercourse that always entails sin. He cannot perfect himself by piously withdrawing; he will achieve no self unless he opens himself to other men. What he is depends on what he does for others, for the world, finally for God.

Psychology leads necessarily to ethics, ethics to politics, politics to the question of the Messiah. For a Jew, God is more than "the ground of our being," in Paul Tillich's phrase. He is the One who makes us able to be man. While Freud helps us understand our tensions, Buber illuminates our potential. Freud makes us see man in his limiting, destructive dynamics. Buber helps us know how man can rise through biological and psychic mechanisms to become a person.

The Jewish idea of man, through the vision of these modern thinkers, provides no comfort for sinners, no evasion of the real task. But, perhaps, the Torah* can teach us to find hope, not by taking us out of the immoral world we all have made, but precisely in God's command to turn back to Him, a command which implies man has the power to turn. For Judaism, what man is depends on what he becomes. Under God, man is the maker of man.

Every Jewish source is, of course, about man. The Bible is not a God-book—it is a man-book, a story of real (dreadfully, wonderfully real) men. The Talmud ** is a book for men by men. It is the record of how many men in many decades wrestled with the problem of what man must do and also with one another's insights and idiosyncracies. While the New Testament tends to be about persons who are, to say the least, highly unusual, the Hebrew Bible, the Talmud and other classics of Jewish thought deal with real individuals. Jewish philosophers and poets over the millennia have also been physicians, statesmen, neighbors. They have cared about man. Jewish mystics thought to serve God by becoming men.

The entire Torah is a Torah of men. Some small samplings are here translated and brought together in this volume, which deals with the Jewish view of man.

Judaism sees man as a paradox. Man's life is central, but it is also weak, absurd. Man is the highest point of creation; he is also doomed to death. Man is inclined to good and can study and obey Torah; he is also weakened by his evil inclination, his

* Narrowly, the first five books of the Bible, the Teaching of Moses, but, by extension, all the Jewish tradition which derives from them.

** The classic record of rabbinic discussions on the basic post-Biblical code of laws, the Mishnah and Gemara were compiled about 500 C.E. and contain the chief record of the traditions of the previous six centuries.

Yetzer Hara. He is given a good world to enjoy by a good God; but he must also renounce much of what tempts him. He is immortal or can become worthy of his resurrection; but death is still a terror and a fact.

Indeed, man remains a mystery: he is more than he seems. He is the image of God; he points to God. He shares God's grandeur, though he is far less grand. He shares the mystery, though he is far less wondrous.

While some religions are God-religions that glory in their theogenies and theologies and others are man-religions which worship man as all-in-all, Judaism is a God-and-man religion. It is a covenant faith, in which man finds his meaning precisely and uniquely under God, but in which God, too, needs man's love. As God is both transcendent and immanent, both far and near, so man is close to Him and yet infinitely removed. Our closeness is our glory, our distance our tragedy. Man mysteriously unites both glory and tragedy, both life and death, both good and evil.

Judaism does not tell us explicitly what man is. But it tells us with great precision what man must do: he must love and help men; he must love and serve God. In our task is our definition. What we perform is, with God's help, what we may someday come to be.

CONTENTS

WHAT IS MAN?

1

Man: Battleground of Good and Evil

The grandest, most imposing and in many ways most important collection of Jewish books is the Talmud. Produced during the first six centuries of the Common Era, it contains laws, stories, argument and Biblical interpretation. The passage we translate here from *Tractate Sukkah* (on the laws of The Feast of Booths), includes some of each of these. It interprets a number of Biblical passages, some literally, many freely, almost all brilliantly. It reproduces the debates of learned rabbis on several important subjects. It tells what is supposed to have happened to many people: never simply for the story's sake, but always for the purpose of suggesting a deeper truth.

The subject is, in effect, the nature of man. Man, according to these Rabbis, is divided within himself. His most basic drives are evil, leading him to lust, passion, desire for possession. His *Yetzer Hara*, Evil Inclination, is at the very core of his being. It is irrevocable, ineluctable, and (except, perhaps, in some future time under God's special decree) indestructible.

But man also possesses a *Yetzer Tov*, a Good Inclination. It wrestles with evil for mastery, it turns him toward his Father's way and will. Though it tries to make man obedient and chaste, the very struggle may also cripple and destroy him.

This analysis of our human structure suggests a number of problems. The text does not "answer" any of them, but it does illuminate them. Is the Evil Inclination wholly or chiefly "bad"? Does it not furnish man with the fuel necessary for his internal combustion machinery, in the manner of Freud's id? Is the Evil

Inclination omnipotent or weak? Do different men have differing kinds of Evil Inclinations? Does the saint have the smallest *Yetzer* or the greatest one which he has somehow transformed and mastered?

Is the Evil Inclination dynamic—that is, does it grow as it acts within a person or between persons? If what becomes of it depends on what we do about it, how should we treat our passions: by renunciation, by sublimation, by manipulation? Are Jews more or less subject than other men to instinctual urges? To what extent is Judaism a way of dealing not only with the evil that befalls us, but also with the evil we discover within ourselves?

Perhaps the Evil Inclination is necessary. In any case, all men possess it. The tragic story of Adam's sin in the Garden of Eden may well signify that the only way to be human is to be permamently subject to desire. God may have had to make us what we are if He wanted to make men at all. He must have known that our inclination to evil would be at least as strong as our inclination to good.

Life is good, but it always embraces evil. God loves man, but the man He loves is no saint. Man, according to the Rabbis, is less than he often pretends to be. He can become "good," but only at a price and never wholly. He performs evil over and over again because some part of him will not be transformed.

At least, not until that Messianic time described in the passage that follows. On that day, say our teachers, God will be One and His Name One. Then, too, will man be healed and whole. Until then he struggles toward his own survival and integrity.

FROM

Talmud

(*Tractate Sukkah, 51b–52a,b*)

Our Rabbis taught: At one time the women used to sit in their
own court in the Temple while the men were outside. But this
led to some irresponsible behavior, so the women were seated
outside and the men inside. Since this still caused levity, however,
it was finally required for the women to sit a level up, in their
own gallery, with the men below.

How were they permitted to alter the structure of the Temple?
Was it not ordained in the Bible: *All this law for the building
of the Temple I give thee in writing as the Lord hath enlightened
me with His own hand upon me.* God Himself had ordained it!

Rab replied: they found another Biblical verse and used it as
a basis for their change: *And the land shall mourn, the family
of the house of David apart and their wives apart.* They argued
from the less to the more obvious. If even in that Messianic
future of which the verse speaks, when the Evil Inclination will
no longer have power over men, so that levity would hardly be
likely—if even in that time the Bible speaks of the separation
of men and women, then how much the more so now, when
certain gay Temple services take place and the Evil Inclination
rules people, must we keep men and women separate?

What is the cause of the mourning to take place in the distant
future which our verse has mentioned? Rabbi Dosa and the other
Rabbis differ in their answers. He holds that it refers to mourning when the preliminary Messiah, not of the Davidic family
but of the tribes descended from Joseph, will be killed. The
other Rabbis interpret it to be a result of the future destruction
of man's Evil Inclination.

The first interpretation presents no special difficulties, since it could well be applied to the neighboring verse of the Bible: *They shall look upon me as one mourning for his only son.* When the Messiah, son of Joseph, is killed, the sad occasion could well produce deep mourning.

But what about the other interpretation? If the Evil Inclination will be rooted out of man and destroyed, why should there be any mourning at all? Would that not more logically be an occasion for joy? Why should anyone weep at the final destruction of the Evil Inclination?

Rabbi Judah tried to explain why by this story: In days to come the Holy One, blessed be He, will bring out the Evil Inclination and kill it in the presence of both the righteous and the wicked. To the righteous their Evil Impulse will look like a high hill. To the wicked it will seem as small as a lock of hair. Both of them will weep. The righteous will say through their tears: "How were we able to overcome such a high hill!" The wicked will say in deep shame, "How could we have been unable to conquer even this slender hair!" And the Holy One, blessed be He, will wonder along with them, as we learn from the Biblical verse: *Thus saith the Lord of Hosts, If it be marvelous in the eyes of the remnant of this people in those days, it shall also be marvelous in My eyes.*

Rabbi Assi said that the Evil Inclination in man is as thin as a spider's web at first, but in the end grows as thick as cartropes. This is hinted at in the verse of Scripture: *Woe unto them that draw iniquity with cords of vanity, and sin as if with a cart-rope.*

Abaye once heard a man say to a woman: "Let us get up early in the morning and take a long walk together." Abaye said to himself, "I will follow them in order to keep them from sexual transgression," and he followed them across the lonely meadows for three miles. When they finally left each other he heard them say, "Our company was pleasant during the long trip together." He was amazed at their restraint and said, "If I had been the man I could not have kept myself away from her!" So he went and leaned against a doorpost in deep anguish. A certain old man came up to him and taught him this about the Evil Inclination: the greater the man, the greater his inclination to evil.

Rabbi Samuel, son of Nahmani, quoting Rabbi Johanan, said: The Evil Inclination entices man to sin in this world and testifies against him in the world to come, as it is said in Scripture: *He that carefully rears a servant from his childhood shall have him become a witness against him in the end.*

Rabbi Huna pointed out an apparent incongruity. One verse says: *For a spirit of harlotry has caused them to err.* But another verse of Scripture says: *The spirit of harlotry is within themselves.* There is no contradiction. First the Evil Inclination only causes men to err, but in the end it becomes a part of them. Rab observed: First the Evil Inclination is called a passer-by, then he is called a guest, and finally he is called a man-at-home, in the Scripture verse: *And there came a passer-by (the Evil Inclination) to the rich man, and he did not want to take of his own flock or herd to dress for this guest.* And then it is written: *He took the poor man's lamb and dressed it for the man who stayed with him.*

Rabbi Hana, son of Abba, stated: It was said at the schoolhouse, there are four things that the Holy One, blessed be He, is sorry He ever made: Exile, the Chaldeans (who destroyed the First Temple), the Romans (who destroyed the Second Temple), and the Evil Inclination. That it is true of the Exile of the Jews we know from the verse: *Now therefore, saith the Lord, what should I do now, since My people has been exiled for nothing!* Of the Chaldeans we read in the Bible: *Behold the land of the Chaldeans, this is the people that was like nothing.* Of the Romans or Ishmaelites it is written: *The tents of the Ishmaelite robbers prosper and they that provoke God are secure since God brought them into His own power.* And of the Evil Inclination it is written: *I will gather her in that I have afflicted* (with the Evil Inclination). So God is actually sorry that He had to make man with an Evil Impulse.

2

Man: Possessor of Life

Some modern critics have accused Judaism of being masochistic. To them, Judaism is basically a life- and pleasure-denying regimen, constricting and painful. Torah means not being allowed to eat this or that, not doing this or that. Discipline implies submitting to a Power beyond oneself. Judaism is not only rigorous, but downright punitive. They find its commandments diminishing, its insights ignoble or simply embarrassing. Judaism is one long painful demand that is impossible, in the end, to live out.

The obvious question is: Why bother? Especially, since to look at Jewish history is to be struck by the continuing record of Jewish suffering: Jews have paid again and again in blood and tears for their beliefs. One need not be a masochist to admit that Judaism costs more than many of us wish to pay. We are supposed to study when we would rather play. We are asked to pray when we would rather nap. We are required to be decent when we might find it easier another way.

Man is not the center of Judaism; God is. And, therefore, man's wants cannot be the final standard, for man is not the measure of all things. He is their inheritor.

Is God, then, man's enemy? Does Judaism narrow our choices and modify our desires only because it wants us to suffer and to die? Does it consider man a worthless child of a strict Father, or, even worse, the ungrateful slave of a vicious Master? Does it reduce man to nothing so that God can be everything? These bitter questions—they are really indictments—have been made by many modern thinkers from Nietzsche to Sartre. Some Jews ask them too, because of their bitter disillusion with life.

Perhaps the central Jewish view of God as a loving, but demanding Father can be found—at least partially—in the following two selections taken from the *Kitzur Shulhan Arukh,* an abridgement of the monumental code of Jewish law written by Rabbi Joseph Karo in the sixteenth century. Karo himself was a remarkable blend of mystic and legalist, visionary and man of affairs. His code came to be the practical guide to Orthodox Judaism in more recent centuries. Though it lacks the dialectical fascination of the Talmud or the scholarly subtleties of Maimonides, Karo's book has its own merits. It tells simply and fully what Judaism says about holidays and marriage, about loans and torts and "cabbages and kings." In the selections presented here, it tells what Judaism says about the dying and the dead. The shorter version of Karo's code which we quote was made by the Hungarian rabbi and scholar, Solomon Ganzfried, about a hundred years ago, and has been frequently reprinted and translated. It may well be the most useful single book traditional Jews possess.

Judaism puts the saving of life ahead of almost every other commandment. The *Kitzur Shulhan Arukh* details the priority but does not argue for it. We are obliged to infer the theory behind the law. It tells us that respect must be paid even to a person who is dying or to a man who has died; we must intuit what this signifies for the nature of man. Men sicken and die, all men; about this Judaism has no illusions. But men who are sick remain men; corpses are still men. And to be a man is to have dignity and to command respect.

FROM

Kitzur Shulhan Arukh

Law about a sick person in danger of dying and about someone who is obliged to sin in order to save his life

1. When there is mortal danger if one obeys the law, then, as with all commandments of the Torah, the Sabbath law is abrogated. If a man is sick and in danger of dying one must violate the Sabbath to help him, even if he has sometimes sinned out of passion or even if he is only a day-old baby. If the sick person will not allow us to help him, we force him to accept treatment, because it is sinful to refuse to be healed on account of a lesser law. Of him (such a pious fool) the Torah says: *I will surely require your blood for your souls.*

It is proper to violate the Sabbath to help a dangerously sick person. Even if there is a Gentile present who could do the work on Sabbath, we prefer to ask a Jew. Anyone who violates the Sabbath for a dangerously sick person will be rewarded, even if it proves to have been unnecessary. If, for example, a doctor prescribed a fig and nine men ran to get one, God will reward each of them, even if the very first fig cured the patient.

This applies to every case where there is danger of death, even doubtful ones. To save a life every law in the Torah may be violated. Nothing comes before human life; the Torah was given precisely for life, as it is said: *These are laws by which a man shall live.* The commentators explain: The Torah is to live by and not to die for. Only idolatry, prohibited sexual relationships and murder are in the category of "die rather than violate these laws!"

2. We take the word of anyone who claims that a person is dangerously sick, even without consulting professionals, and we

violate the Sabbath for that patient. We believe a physician even if he only *thinks* it is a case of grave danger, because where human life is at stake, we must take no chances. If another physician or the patient himself discounts the danger, we accept the opinion of the physician who is more cautious. If the patient says he needs a certain medicine and his physician disagrees, we accept the patient's view. However, if the physician says that the medicine is actually harmful, we listen to him.

3. If a trained physician, Jew or Gentile, says that a patient in no immediate danger might grow much worse unless we give him medicine, the Sabbath must be violated, even if the patient says he does not need medicine. If a physician says that without the medicine the patient will die, while with it he has a bare chance to live, we violate the Sabbath to get the medicine.

4. To treat an internal wound, inside the lips (including the teeth), a lesion or boil, we violate the Sabbath without professional diagnosis, even if the patient is silent. We act as if it were a weekday. But if professional opinion is certain that the illness is not in need of immediate treatment, we do not violate the Sabbath. Discomfort as such is not a disease, but a tooth-ache that makes the body ache may be cured by a non-Jewish dentist on Sabbath.

5. We must violate the Sabbath to treat a lesion on the back of the hand or foot, a wound caused by an iron instrument, hemorrhoids, a swallowed leech, the bite of a rabid dog or a snake (even if we are not sure that it is poisonous), or a very high fever. But to treat ordinary illness, a non-Jewish physician should be called.

6. We must treat high blood-pressure immediately, and, even in the summer, keep warm a patient who is in shock.

7. We violate the Sabbath to treat pain or injury to the eyes, watering or bleeding or pus.

8. If a dangerously sick patient needs meat and we have only forbidden meat, we slaughter an animal even on the Sabbath for him so that eating forbidden food will not make him sick to his stomach. But if the patient is a child or is unaware and hysterical

so that there is no fear of nausea, we feed him forbidden meat, and no animal should be slaughtered on Sabbath.

9. A person who is well must not eat food made for an invalid until the Sabbath is over—and then only if a Jew cooked it.

10. We do not violate the Sabbath to save someone from committing a sin under compulsion, no matter how grave the sin. But we do, in order to keep a Jew, or even a Jewish child, from being forced to convert to another religion. We act on the Sabbath for him just as vigorously as we would for a dangerously ill person, since the Torah says: *The children of Israel shall keep the Sabbath.* Our teachers comment: Violate one Sabbath that he may keep many. We do what we can even if our effort may ultimately be useless, just as we do for a sick patient who may die. But we do not break the Sabbath for a Jew who wants to convert. Since he has chosen deliberately, we cannot ask someone else to "sin in order to keep your fellow-Jew from sinning." Still, some authorities say that to save even a deliberate apostate we may break a Jewish law based on rabbinic though not direct Biblical authority, like walking too far, or riding or handling money on the Sabbath.

FROM

Kitzur Shulhan Arukh

Law about a dying person and the watching of the corpse

1. A dying person is considered a living person in every respect. Therefore, it is forbidden to handle him in any way which might hasten his death, as in the way that touching a feeble flame might extinguish it. Even if he has been dying for a long time, which causes agony to him and his family, it is still forbidden to accelerate his death by removing his pillows or by putting synagogue keys under his head: all such behavior is forbidden. But

if something is retarding his death like a repeated sound, it is permitted to remove it, since that would not directly kill him, but only remove an obstacle which does not require handling the patient.

2. Even though it is forbidden to touch a dying person, still, if the house catches fire, he must not be left to die, but must be brought out. He is removed even before any sacred books that may be in the house are removed.

3. The people who stand around a dying person must take pains not to allow any part of his body to extend beyond the bed, as we know from Jacob: *He gathered his feet into the bed.* Accordingly, they stand chairs around the bed, so that he cannot put a hand or foot outside. But if he does, it is forbidden to touch him in order to put his limb back.

4. When a person is at the point of dying, one should not leave him, so that he not die alone, for the soul is afraid when it leaves the body. It is a commandment to be with a person when he dies, as it is said in the Book of Psalms: *He shall live forever and not see destruction, for he shall see the wise die.* It is appropriate to gather ten men at the death-bed. They are not there to gossip, but to study Torah, read Psalms and other prayers from a book like *Jabbok's Ford.** Candles are lit in the presence of the dying.

5. After death, they are to place a little feather near the nostrils of the dead man. If it does not move, they know he is dead. Then the windows are opened and the mourners say the prayer after a relative who has died. When they reach the blessing, "Blessed be God, righteous Judge," they say the Divine Name and make a tear in their clothing as a sign of mourning.

6. All those who stand around a person when he dies must tear their garments, too. (One mourns similarly the burning of a Torah scroll.) If a child who has studied only a verse of Scripture or if a woman dies, they must likewise rend their garments. Even if the dead man had sometimes sinned out of lust, they tear their clothing for him. But if he was an habitual sinner and belongs to

* A medieval devotional anthology.

the group that has separated from the ways of the Jewish community, they need not tear their clothes for him. Those who are not part of the mourning family, but only happened to be present when the person died, need only make a small rip in their hem or lapel.

7. The eyes of a corpse are closed. If he had a son, the son must close his father's eyes as Joseph did for Jacob. If there is more than one son, the oldest must do it.

8. When they take him off his death-bed and lay him on the ground, they must be careful to keep him dressed because all proprieties owed to a living person apply to a corpse.

9. It is a custom to pour out any water found in vessels in the three houses closest to the dead person's including his own, even if the deceased was a baby less than thirty days old. On the Sabbath it is not necessary to pour out the water.

10. The person who watches over the corpse until the funeral, even if he is not a relative, is released from the obligatory daily prayers and all the other commandments of the Torah, for while he is performing one commandment he is exempt from the others. If there are two watchers, however, one watches over the corpse while the other prays.

11. It is forbidden to eat in a room in which a corpse is present unless the room is partitioned; even a snack or a piece of fruit or a drink of water is forbidden. Watchmen should be warned about this. And no blessing may be pronounced in the room.

12. It is forbidden to handle a corpse, even of a priest, on the Sabbath, or even for the sake of performing a commandment. It may be done by a Gentile, however, with the family's permission.

3

Man: Partner of God

In the Bible man's dignity is rooted in his relationship to God. He is God's creature, God's servant, God's child.

But serving God, for all of that, is no easy task. Most of the early stories in the Bible tell how the first fathers lost their way and sinned. Much of the Book is about Israel's sin, about Jews turning away from God.

Yet the Bible is not hopeless or cynical. It does not give up on man. It affirms and reaffirms that there is a way from man to God. The servant is never dismissed nor the son disowned. Sometimes the way is called *tz'dakah,* righteousness; sometimes Torah, instruction; sometimes *t'shuvah,* turning. The community is commanded, convoked, chosen. And every man has the task himself of choosing to live before God.

Perhaps the most personal statement of the human task is found in the Book of Psalms. In the smooth poetry of the King James English Bible, the Psalms seem inspiring and uplifting. But in the Hebrew, *T'hillim* are also turbulent and challenging. They reflect less the still waters than the passionate journey, less the pure Oneness of God than the divided, suffering heart of man. Some psalms, as an old rabbinic comment notes, are *mizmor l'David,* a song that God, in effect, gives to David. But most are *l'David mizmor,* a song of David, man's own song.

The man who sings in the Psalms is not a saint. He is one who needs God. He knows the only path to Him is righteousness, and being righteous is hard. The psalmist does not usually boast of his spiritual triumph; more often he is picking himself up out of the dust where his folly has brought him. He is not a stained-glass spiritual giant. Like all men he is weak, aspiring, confused, rarely triumphant. But he hungers for God.

The psalmist knows that what counts with God is what men do. There is no substitute for obedience. Only by doing what God wants can man please God or be made human by Him. Humanity, for the psalmist, is the struggle for rightness. His heroes are not soldiers but do-gooders, not merchants or lovers or scientists but men whose vocation is following God's path. The only success the psalmist acknowledges is faithfulness to the task. The only happiness for which he longs is the hope that somehow he has not failed God.

Money cannot bribe the psalmist though he knows the agonies of being poor. Pleasure is more appealing: this we know from the seductive images of his poetry. But doing God's pleasure alone brings joy. The psalmist's paean to righteousness goes far to explain the loyalty of generations of Jews to God, and their communities' struggle for conformity to His will.

But knowing the centrality of goodness is only half of what the psalmist knows of man. He also knows that while some men are good, some are evil. He knows, too, that good men are both good and evil, that evil men often succeed while good men fail. What looks like success is often failure, and a life made up wholly of failures may yet be a success. Men must die and death hovers over life. But the psalmist expects something from God, somewhere, some time, that death cannot destroy. He is a realist without sacrificing his heart's desire. Sometimes he comes to God joyfully and proud. But sometimes he comes ashamed of his sin, conscious of his unworthiness. Sometimes he is unable to come to Him at all. Yet trusting Him, not himself, he does come.

At such moments the psalmist is deeply aware not only of specific, redeemable sins, but also of sin, that nameless guilt which haunts all men. Christianity turned this into a teaching about Original Sin which remains distinct from the original Jewish doctrine of sin and atonement. The latter is subtle and must be studied in connection with other passages in the Psalms and throughout the Bible. The Jewish view denies categorically any modern notion of man which says he does not need God or God's forgiveness, or that God and His forgiveness are not directly available to man. The psalmist feels man needs forgiveness. And he knows God hears and forgives. That is his uniquely Jewish faith.

Some men even in Biblical times denied the sovereignty of God (not through philosophy, but probably by deed). The psalmist thinks such men stupid, blind, wicked. To live without God is to deny standards, values, goals. It is to say everything is permissible, which, for man, is a way of committing suicide. And the psalmist chooses life.

But how does the "good," good-bad, sinful-repentant man ever really find God? Through the alchemy of prayer, the therapy of turning, the discipline of Torah? By abandoning reliance on his own power? By seeking love and righteousness? By doing all he can for man and then trusting God to do what only He can do for us?

The Psalms are poetry, great poetry. They do not tell us what to do in the manner of the Talmud or the Codes. Nor do they elucidate a system. They are, even the greatest of them, but fragments of a whole. Some of the most evocative are but fragments of a fragment. It does not matter that they do not preach; they sing. Sometimes a phrase, sometimes only a word instructs as it cleanses. Yet in the outreach their prayer before God becomes in itself a teaching about man.

FROM

Book of Psalms

One

Happy is the man who has
        not walked in wicked men's counsel
Who has not stood in sinful men's road

Who has not sat where cynics sit.
But lusts for God's Torah.
And he studies His Torah day and night.
He is like a tree planted where waters meet
Yielding its fruit each season,
Whose leaf does not wither.
Whatever he may do will succeed.

It is not so with wicked men.
They are like chaff driven away by the wind.
That is why evil men must not
              rise to power
Nor sinful men be included in the
              assembly of righteous men.
For God loves the road of
              righteous men
But the road of evil men
              leads nowhere.

Eight

Adonai, our Lord, how glorious is Your Name in the whole earth,
Who fixed Your Glory above the heaven.
From what children say, nurselings,
You build strength against Your enemies,
To stop the enemy and the vengeful.

If I look at Your Heaven, the work of Your fingers
Moon or stars that You created,
What is man that You should remember him?
What is man that You should deal with him?
But You left him lower only than angels,
You garlanded him with significance and beauty.
You gave him rule over what Your hands made
Putting everything under his feet,
Sheep, oxes, all of them, all the beasts of field, birds of the air,
Fish of the sea, that pass through the seas' streets.

Adonai, our Lord, how glorious is Your Name in the whole earth.

Fifteen: A Psalm of David

God, who can live in Your tent?
Who can dwell on Your holy hill?

The man who walks with integrity
And speaks truly from his heart.
Who is not quick with his tongue
Nor does wrong to his neighbor
Nor takes his neighbor's blame.
In his eyes a bad man is despicable,
But he takes God-fearing men seriously.
He keeps his promise though it hurt
And takes no interest on a loan.
Nor a bribe against the innocent.

A man who acts this way
      is immovable.

Twenty-Four: A Psalm of David

God's is the world and what fills it.
The earth and those who live on it.
For He founded it on the seas
He balanced it on the ocean-currents.

Who may go up to God's mountain?
Who may rise to His holy place?
One with clean hands and a pure heart
Who has not sought falsehood
Nor sworn to a lie.

He will earn blessing from God
And fairness from the God who
      saves him.
This is what a generation is like
      that seeks Him
That seeks Your face, O God of Jacob.

Thirty-Six: For the Director: Of David, God's Slave

In my heart
        is an oracle of the evil man's sin,
Of him, who has no fear of God before his eyes.
His eyes deceive him, prevent him
        from finding and hating his sin.
The words of his mouth are wrong.
He has stopped understanding
        and doing good.
He plans crime in bed.
He takes his stand on a road
        that is not good.
He does not despise evil.

God, Your faithful love
        is in heaven.
Your loyalty in the clouds.
Your justice like the highest mountains,
Your power a great deep.
Man and beast You save, God.
How precious is Your love, God,
Under the shadow of Your wings
        men take refuge.
They drink their fill of the best
        of Your house.
You give them drink of
        Your pleasant stream.
For with You is the source of life
In Your light we see light.

Continue Your love to those who love You
And Your justice to the fair-minded.
Let not pride's foot come against me
Nor the hand of evil men drive me out.
Somewhere evil-doers have fallen,
Are overthrown and cannot rise.

Forty-Nine: For the Director:
A Psalm of the Sons of Korah

Hear this, all peoples.
Pay attention, all dwellers on earth,
Men's sons, mankind
Rich and poor together:
My mouth would speak wisely
My heart's meditation insight.
I shall turn my ear to a parable
I shall open with a mystery
            in music.

Why should I fear in bad days
When my guilty foes surround me,
Those who trust in their wealth
And boast of their great riches?
None of them can buy his brother back
Or bribe God.
It is too expensive
To ransom a person
That one might live forever
And not see destruction.

He sees it! Wise men die,
Fools and knaves die, too,
And leave their wealth to others.
Their graves are their eternal homes
Their dwelling-places for generations to come,
Plots of sand called by their name.

Man with his honor cannot abide
He is like the animals that perish.

This is the road of their folly
The end of men who like what they themselves say:
They are buried like sheep.
Death will be their Shepherd.

In the morning good men will walk on them
As their body decays in the grave.

But God will ransom me
        from the grave
And will take me.

Fear not if a man grows rich,
If the splendor of
        his home increases.
He will take nothing with him
        in death.
His glory will not follow him down
He would say a blessing just to be alive
And congratulate you for your
        good fortune.
Because you go on to his son's generation
While he sees light no more.

Man understands nothing.
He is like the animals that die.

Fifty-One: For the Director: David's Psalm When Nathan the Prophet Came to Him After He Had Seduced Bathsheba

Pity me, God, in Your love
Blot out my sins in Your great compassion
Wash me of my sin
Make me clean of my failures.
For I know my sins
My failures always face me.
My sin is against You only,
I have done evil in Your eyes.
So You are right when You speak,
When You judge,
        Your verdict is correct.

I was born in guilt.
My mother conceived me in sin.

You have wanted truth.
You help me know wisdom accurately.
Purge me with hyssop that I may be clean.
Wash me whiter than snow.
Let me hear joy.
Let the bones You broke exult.
Hide Your face from my sin.
Wipe out all my failures.
Create a pure heart for me, God
Renew a steady spirit in me.
Do not hurl me from You.
Do not take Your holy spirit from me.
Bring back to me the joy of Your salvation,
Uphold me with a giving spirit.
Let me teach sinners Your way
That those who fail may turn to You.
Save me from blood, God, God who
            saves me,
Let my tongue sing Your right.

Adonai, open my lips,
Let my mouth tell Your praise.
For You do not want sacrifice or I
            would give it,
You do not enjoy holocausts.
The sacrifices of God are a broken spirit,
A broken, lonely heart, God, You
            will not scorn.
Do good for Zion graciously,
Build Jerusalem's walls
Where You will want true offerings,
Then they may send up animals on
            Your altar.

Fifty-Three: For the Director:
A Wise Poem of David
Upon an Instrument

A stupid man believes there
    is no God,
Deceivers who do no good.
God looks down from heaven on men,
To see if there is any thoughtful man
    seeking God.
Each one deserts, befouls
    himself
None does good, not one.
Do not the evil-doers who eat
    up my people as bread know?
Have they never called "God"?
They were very fearful where
No terror was.
For God scattered your enemy's bones.
You have made fools of those whom
    God rejected.
May Israel's salvation come from Zion!
When God makes his people turn.
Jacob shall rejoice, Israel be glad.

Sixty-Two: For the Director:
A Psalm of David Upon an Instrument

Only for God do I silently wait
From Him is my salvation.
Only He is my rock and my salvation,
My Tower from which I shall not
    move far away.

How long will you wait for a man
To murder him, all of you
Like a leaning fence, a breaking wall?

They only plot to put one down from
        his height,
They enjoy lying,
They bless God with their mouths
And curse Him inside.

My soul, be still only for God
For my hope is from Him
Only He is my rock and my salvation,
My Tower from which I shall not move.

My real salvation depends on God,
On my strong rock, my refuge, God.
Trust Him always, people,
Pour your heart out to Him,
God is our refuge.

Man is wind, a lie is man,
On a scale lighter than wind,
Do not trust oppression.
Do not stupidly hope in robbery.
Do not seek foolishly to get rich.
Do not set your heart on it.

God told us several things:
That power is God's
Yours, God, is love,
And You pay a man for his work.

Ninety: A Prayer of Moses, God's Man

Adonai, You have been our
        dwelling place in each generation.
Before mountains were born or You formed
        the earth, the world.
From eternity to eternity You are God.
You turn man back to dust
        You say: return men!

For a thousand years in
        Your eyes are yesterday
                when it is past,
A watch in night.
You cut them off.
They are like sleep.
In the morning they grow like
        grass.
In the morning it shoots up,
In the evening it withers and dies.
We are destroyed by Your rage
By Your wrath worn out.
You have set our sins before You.
Our secret is clear to You.
All our days have passed in
        Your anger,
Our years have blown away like a sigh.

Our life-span is seventy years
With health, eighty years.
But their length is work and sin
For it is soon cut off and
        we fly away.
Who knows how strong Your anger is?
Does our fear of You befit Your wrath?
So teach us to count our days
That we may get a wise mind.
Turn, God—how long?
Pity Your servants.
Fill us with Your love in the morning
That we may be glad through all our days.
Give us joy for the days You have
        hurt us,
The years we have seen evil.
May Your work appear to Your servants
Your splendor to their children.

May *Adonai,* our God's favor,
      be upon us.
Establish for us the work of our
      hands,
Establish the work of our hands.

One Hundred One:
A Psalm of David

I sing of love and justice,
To You, God, I sing.
I think of the way of integrity.
When will You come to me?
I walk in my heart's integrity
      within my house.
I do not
      look for crime.
I hate evil-doing,
It will not cling to me.
A perverse heart repels me
I do not understand evil.
One who slanders his neighbor
      in secret
          I cut.

The proud, high-minded man
      I cannot endure.
My eyes are on the earth's
      faithful
Who live with me.
A man who walks straight
      can serve me.
One who acts deceitfully
      may not live in my house.
One who tells lies
      will not stay in my sight.

Mornings I'll destroy the
    earth's wicked
Cutting off from God's city
    all evil-doers.

One Hundred Twenty-Seven:
Solomon's Song

If God does not build a house
Those who build work in vain.
If God does not guard a city,
The watchman stays awake for nothing.
Uselessly you get up early, stay up late,
Eat hard-earned bread.
He gives His loved ones sleep.

Children are God's heritage
The fruit of the womb a reward.
Like arrows in a hero's hand
Are the children of youth.
Happy is the man with a
        quiver full of them.
He will not be ashamed
        to speak to his
                enemies in town.

One Hundred Twenty-Eight:
A Song

Happy is everyone who fears God
        and walks in His ways.
You shall eat the labor of your hands.
You shall be happy, all will be well.
Your wife will be a fruitful vine
        within your house.
Your children olive-trees
        around your table.

Thus blessed is the man who fears God.
May God bless you from Zion.
May you see the good of Jerusalem
        all your life's days.
May you see grandchildren
        and peace upon Israel.

One Hundred Thirty:
A Song

From the depths I call You, God.
Adonai, hear my voice
Let Your ears attend the voice of
        my supplication.

If You recorded sins, God, who
        could stand?
But You forgive
That You may be worshipped.

I wait for God, my whole being waits,
And for His word I hope.
I wait for God
More than watchmen for morning,
More than watchmen for morning.

Hope, Israel, in God
For with God is love and great
        freedom.
He will free Israel of all its guilt.

4

Man: Servant of God

The book most read by generations of Jews, most beloved and most revelatory, is neither the Bible, which is a small library, nor the encyclopedic Talmud. It is the Prayerbook, which is more like an anthology. The Prayerbook contains Biblical and Talmudic selections, prose and poetry, original meditations and anonymous exclamation, ideas to study and lyrics to sing, love words between man and God, promises between God and the people of Israel. God is the "Thou" who is also "He," the One addressed, the One beyond man's power to see. The speaker is "I," a single human being, and also "we," the Hebrew folk, and, finally, the whole world of men.

Each morning before he worships with his community (if he can), the pious Jew prays alone in order to be ready to pray. The single Jew addressed or described in the Book of Psalms talks back to God in the *Siddur* (literally, the structure). He spells out his dreams and his needs. The liturgy outlines what he must learn to want: to be used by God. He learns to ask: may Thy will be done.

Perhaps the most scandalous claim of the *Siddur* is that man can bless God: what man says about and does for God affects Him. Man can "make" Him blessed or cursed. What man says and does counts significantly. Man is God's to use, but man determines how he will be used. Only if man submits to God can he himself become a blessing. And only if he struggles to bless God can he learn to submit. It is no accident that most of the early morning prayers (which constitute the texts that follow) are blessings.

As we have seen, the Jewish idea of man is dialectical. On the one hand, man is free: to bless or to curse, to create or to destroy, to love or to die. But he is also part of a divine creation which he did not make and which he can never fully apprehend. Man is for himself, but he is also at God's disposal. Not even God can make him pray or obey; but if he does not he can never learn to use his God-given creativity. Man does not pray to meet his own needs; instead, he learns what it might be to meet God's infinite need.

This task requires above all thankfulness. We are grateful for our veins and our arteries, for the power to learn and the power to wash, for the Torah, for our children and for our parents, for what we have and for what we can give. Most of Jewish prayer is just a poetic way of being grateful. What is clearly implied is that to be a man is to be in debt.

But thanksgiving is not just something man feels. It is something he does: with *tz'dakah,* loving concern for other men's needs; with *t'fillah,* the honest prayer of acknowledgment; with *t'shuvah,* turning back each day to the Source of all gifts, doing.

No contribution of Judaism is more striking or more precious than the Jewish book of common prayer. It has taught most of mankind what to say to God and what it really is to be a man. It sets forth man's right to talk to God and his duty to try.

FROM

Prayerbook

You are blessed, *Adonai,* our God, Master of space and time . . . who made us holy with His commands and commanded us to wash our hands.

You are blessed, *Adonai,* our God, Master of space and time . . . who wisely created man with innumerable vessels and orifices.

You know that if one of these passages were cut open or blocked we could not survive before You. You are blessed, *Adonai*, who keeps flesh healthy in a most wonderful way.

You are blessed, *Adonai*, our God, Master of space and time . . . who made us holy with His commands and commanded us to work with Torah-words.

Make the Torah-words pleasant in our mouths and in the mouth of Your people, the house of Israel. May we and our children and our children's children and all Your people's children know Your Name and study Your Torah for the love of it. You are blessed, *Adonai*, teacher of Torah to His people, Israel.

You are blessed, *Adonai*, our God, Master of space and time . . . who chose us from among all peoples by giving us His Torah. You are blessed, *Adonai*, the Giver of Torah.

I now fulfill my minimal daily obligation to study the Bible: *May* Adonai *bless you and keep you. May* Adonai *make His face shine toward you and be kind to you. May* Adonai *lift His face toward you and give you integrity.*

I now fulfill my minimal daily obligation to study the Talmud: *These responsibilities have no upper limit: the corner of the field that must be left to the poor, the gift of first fruits, the pilgrimage offering, acts of covenant-love, study of Torah. Of the following you enjoy the dividends in this world and the principle remains for the life to come: honoring father and mother, acts of covenant-love, studying Judaism early and late, welcoming a stranger, visiting the sick, dowering a bride, accompanying the dead to the grave, concentrating in prayer, bringing peace between man and man. And the study of Torah leads to them all.*

My God, the self which you gave me is pure. You made it. You breathed it into me. You keep it in my body. You will take it from me and give it back to me in time to come. While there is still self within me I thank You, *Adonai*, my God and my father's

God, Master of all selves. You are blessed, *Adonai,* who restores selfhood to corpses.

You are blessed, *Adonai,* our God, Master of space and time . . . who gave the cock enough understanding to distinguish day from night.

You are blessed, *Adonai,* our God, Master of space and time . . . who did not make me a pagan.

You are blessed, *Adonai,* our God, Master of space and time . . . who did not make me a slave.

(Men say:) You are blessed, *Adonai,* our God, Master of space and time . . . who did not make me a woman.

(Women say:) You are blessed, *Adonai,* our God, Master of space and time . . . who made me as He pleased.

You are blessed, *Adonai,* our God, Master of space and time . . . who opens the eyes of the blind.

You are blessed, *Adonai,* our God, Master of space and time . . . who clothes the naked.

You are blessed, *Adonai,* our God, Master of space and time . . . who frees the bound.

You are blessed, *Adonai,* our God, Master of space and time . . . who raises the fallen.

You are blessed, *Adonai,* our God, Master of space and time . . . who stretches the earth over the water.

You are blessed, *Adonai,* our God, Master of space and time . . . who provides for my every need.

You are blessed, *Adonai,* our God, Master of space and time . . . who guides man's steps.

You are blessed, *Adonai,* our God, Master of space and time . . . who clothes Israel in power.

You are blessed, *Adonai,* our God, Master of space and time . . .
who garbs Israel in glory.

You are blessed, *Adonai,* our God, Master of space and time . . .
who gives the weary strength.

You are blessed, *Adonai,* our God, Master of space and time . . .
who takes sleep away from my eyes and slumber from my eyelids.

May it be Your will, *Adonai,* our God and our fathers', to make
me walk in Your Torah, to make me cling to Your commands.
Do not bring us into the power of sin, temptation or disgrace.
Do not let an Evil Inclination rule over us. Keep us far from a
bad man and a bad friend. Make us cling to the Good Inclination with good deeds. Bend our Inclination to serve You. This
day and each day give us love, trust and mercy in Your eyes and
in the eyes of all who see us. Favor us with covenant-love. You
are blessed, *Adonai,* who bestows covenant-love on His people
Israel.

May it be Your will, *Adonai,* my God and my fathers' God, to
save me this day and each day from insolent people and from
insolence, from a bad man, a bad friend, a bad neighbor and a
bad experience, and from a hinderer or a destroyer, from a harsh
judgment and a harsh adversary, whether he be a son of the covenant or not.

Our God and our fathers' God, remember us for good. From the
eternal heights of heaven, remember us with thoughts of mercy
and salvation. *Adonai,* our God, remember us in the light of the
love of our patriarchs, Abraham, Isaac and Israel, Your servants.
Recall for us the covenant and covenant-love, the oath You swore
to Abraham, our father, on Mount Moriah, the binding of Isaac,
his son, on the altar, as is written in Your Torah. Master of
space and time, may it be Your will, *Adonai,* our God and our
fathers', to remember for us Your covenant with our fathers. As
Abraham our father mastered his compassion for his only son
in order to do Your will with a whole heart, so may Your com-

passion master Your anger at us. May Your mercy temper Your justice. Give us the benefit of the doubt when Your mercy and Your justice confront us. In Your great mercy, let Your wrath be turned from Your people, Your city, Your land, and Your heritage. Fulfill for us, *Adonai,* our God, what You promised Moses, Your servant, as is recorded in Scripture: *I shall remember My covenant with Jacob and My covenant with Isaac and My covenant with Abraham, and I shall remember the land.*

A man should always fear God in private and in public, acknowledging the truth and telling himself the truth. Let him get up early in the morning and say: Master of all worlds, not because of our victories do we supplicate You, but only because of Your great compassion. What are we? What is our life? What is our loyalty? What is our triumph? What is our help? What is our strength? What is our power? What can we say to You, our God and our fathers'? Are not all powerful men nothing before You, and men of renown as though they had not existed, and wise men as if without knowledge, and perceptive men as if without insight? Most of their deeds are empty, and the days of their lives are vanity to You. The superiority of man over beast is nothing. Everything is vanity.

But we are Your people, children of Your covenant, children of Abraham who loved You, to whom You made a promise on Mount Moriah. We are the seed of Isaac, his first-born son, who was bound on top of the altar. We are the congregation of his first-born son, Jacob, whom You loved and enjoyed and named Israel and Jeshurun.

Therefore we must thank You, praise You, bless and hallow Your Name, and give Your Name thankful praise. How fortunate we are! How good is our portion! How pleasant is our lot! How beautiful is our heritage! How fortunate it is for us to be able to say early in the morning and late at night, twice each day:

> Hear, Israel, *Adonai,* is our God, *Adonai* alone.
> Blessed be His glorious and sovereign Name for
> ever and ever.

You were before the world was created and now that the world has been created. You are in this world, and You are in the coming world. Make Your Name holy to those who hallow Your Name. Make Your Name holy in Your whole world. With Your saving power raise us to power. You are blessed, *Adonai,* who makes Your Name holy among the multitudes.

You are, *Adonai,* our God, in heaven and on earth and in the highest heaven. It is true that You are the first and the last and that besides You there is no god. Gather together from the four corners of the earth those who hope for You. Then all who come into the world will recognize and know that You alone are God over all the kingdoms of the earth. You made heaven and earth, the sea and all that is in them. Who among all You made in the upper or lower worlds could say to You: What are You doing?

Our Father in heaven, deal with us in covenant-love because of Your great Name by which we are called. Keep Your promise, *Adonai,* our God, as recorded in Scripture: *Some day I will bring you in. Some time I will gather you together, and give you a name famous among all the peoples of the earth. That will be when I bring back your captivity before your very eyes,* Adonai *has said.*

5

Man: The Student

The Greek philosophers defined man as an animal that reasons. That is not precisely how the Jewish philosophers see man's superiority over the animals, but it has some connection with their definition. In Judaism, man is not one who reasons or knows, but rather one who studies and tries to know what is ultimately unknowable, at least in part. Man seeks to know God, which he cannot, and God's will, which he can.

Solomon ibn Gabirol lived in the Spanish Golden Age of the eleventh century. He produced liturgical classics and touching personal lyrics in Hebrew. The first neo-Platonic philosopher in Europe, he had an important influence on the Catholic Church. He wrote his philosophic masterpiece *Mekor Hayim* (*Fountain of Life*), which until the nineteenth century was thought to be the work of a Christian called Avicebron.

Gabirol was also interested in psychology and ethics. He edited or invented a group of maxims (a style much favored in his day) which he called *Mivhar Hapeninim* (*Choice of Pearls*). Like pearls they are to be appreciated both individually and as they are strung out together. Here one must read sentence by sentence as well as for the fascination of the whole.

Gabirol, like his contemporary Bahya ibn Pakuda (see next chapter), knows intimately the dialectics of good and evil. He is not afraid to show up human self-serving in all its pettiness and squalor. He asks which man is truly wise: the one who has or the one who is? In a golden time of a golden land, Gabirol looks toward a better time and a better world. His instruction is harsh, sometimes too repressive for our modern tastes, but his wisdom is never foolish.

Modern philosophers seem to fall into the errors of the extreme. Either they make human reason their god and insist that only man's intellectual apparatus is worthy of him, or they deny that reason is anything but rationalization. Either they try to be "rational" even about love and death, mystery and life, or they dismiss reason as even a necessary human strategy. Either they claim to know or they refuse to learn.

Gabirol in the chapter on wisdom, which follows, asks us to study. Why? Not because we shall ever know everything or because we shall know anything for sure. Science throws up two questions for every solution it claims. Philosophy fights each generation over the same battlegrounds as did preceding generations, and for the same scraps of intellectual treasure. Gabirol knows from his master Plato that all knowing ends only in uncertainty, but with Platonic desperation he still seeks to learn. Man's mind is not God's, but neither is it a mere animal vestige. Weak as it is, it belongs to him and God expects him to put it to good use.

Man must learn how to learn. He must be systematic, dialogic, humble, patient. If he thinks he needs no teacher (or Teacher) he will gain no wisdom. If he uses his wisdom only to get something for himself, he will never become wise. If he cares too much about pleasure, he will miss the subtle delights of learning. If he is impatient for answers, he will miss the questions that are more important than answers. If he is too proud to admit he does not know, he will never learn to know.

And if he never learns, he will never fully become a man. To Jews of many convictions and many eras, study has always been the most authentic human activity. Memory and inquiry, disciple and master, acceptance and doubt, the past and the present: all have their place in the complex Jewish educational scheme.

Man's discoveries and God's Word humanize. Study cannot do everything, but what it can do cannot be done any other way. In rabbinic fancy even God studies Torah. To what better use could He put His infinite mind and His eternal time?

FROM

Choice of Pearls

BY SOLOMON IBN GABIROL

1. Through wisdom the wise pay in full their obligation to the Creator and man attains the service of God during his lifetime and a good name after his death.

2. There is nothing that sharpens the intellect like instruction in wisdom; there is no truer index to the mind of a wise man than his good conduct.

3. The wise man's question is half of wisdom; a conciliatory attitude toward one's fellow-creatures is half of intelligence; systematic expenditure is half-way to satisfying one's needs.

4. What man is fit to rule? Either a philosopher who has power or a king who seeks wisdom.

5. For him who holds fast to wisdom and righteousness there is no need to fear any man; the righteous fear God alone.

6. Intellectual loss is irrecoverable but wisdom remains with its possessor wherever he turns.

7. Whoever toils in quest of wisdom and instruction acquires laurels; they who are so adorned weave laurels from the gold of their eloquent tongue to set upon the heads of their friends.

8. Whoever toils in quest of wisdom and instruction is prevented from acquiring sins and transgressions, for he is led to despise this transitory world and love a world that is everlasting.

9. In the place of feasting and revelry wisdom does not abide; it is driven away from there.

10. He whom the Creator has endowed with wisdom will not be concerned when distress and trouble befall him; for the

consequence of wisdom is peace and tranquility, but gold and silver buy only distress and trouble.

11. "I search not for wisdom," said the sage, "with the hope of ever coming to the end of it or attaining it completely; rather I search for it so as not to be a fool. The intelligent man should have no other motive than this."

12. The sage exhorted his son: "Be not wise in words, but in deeds, for the wisdom which manifests itself in action will benefit thee in the hereafter, while the wisdom of words remains here."

13. He further exhorted him: "Seat thyself in the presence of the wise, for if thou displayest knowledge they will praise thee, if thou showest thyself a fool they will instruct thee, and should they correct thee, it will be to thine advantage."

14. Fools are prisoners of death; free yourselves from these fetters by wisdom.

15. Were it not for wisdom, we would not seek action; and were it not for action, we would not seek wisdom. Better that I should neglect wisdom because I do not know it than because of my contempt for it.

16. The sage was asked, "How is it thou hast more wisdom than thy fellows?" He replied, "Because I spent more on oil than they spent on wine."

17. A body without wisdom is like a house without a foundation.

18. Whoever is famous for wisdom is respected.

19. Keep silent and you will escape trouble; listen and you will learn.

20. Nothing profits a man so much as to know his status and the degree of his intellectual attainment so that his speech is appropriate to his knowledge.

21. Man is only wise during the time that he searches for wisdom; when he imagines he has completely attained it, he is a fool.

22. Parents can bequeath no more precious heritage to their children than wisdom; for with wisdom a person can acquire

wealth, but out of foolishness they can destroy wealth and be left entirely destitute.

23. If you humble yourself to seek wisdom, you will be honored when others seek it from you.

24. Wisdom is the finest pedigree, love the closest relationship.

25. Kings are the judges of the earth, and wise men are the judges of kings.

26. The wise man enjoys wisdom, the fool folly.

27. How good is the action which wisdom beautifies! How good the wisdom which action beautifies! And how good the action which gentleness beautifies!

28. There is no finer combination than humility and wisdom, power and compassion.

29. Whoever occupies himself with the study of God's law can scarcely be thick-necked or fat.

30. The sage exhorted his son: "Be wise, learn, pay attention, or at least be a lover of wisdom. Be nothing else, lest thou perish."

31. He added: "It is not right to be afraid to ask questions about what thou knowest not for the purpose of gaining knowledge; and when thou art asked concerning what thou knowest not, be not ashamed to say, 'I do not know.'"

32. The superiority of intellect over belief is like the superiority of the head over the body; when the head perishes, the body perishes, and when the intellect perishes, faith perishes.

33. The worth of every man is proportionate to what he knows.

34. If men honor you for your wealth or influence, let it not be pleasing unto you, for the honor will depart when these depart; let it be pleasing to you only if men honor you for your wisdom or piety or teaching.

35. The wise on earth resemble the stars in heaven.

36. The sage was asked: "Who are greater, the wise or the rich?" He replied, "The wise."

37. It was then objected, "If so, how is it that there are more wise men at the doors of the rich than rich men at the doors of

the wise?" He replied, "Because the wise appreciate the advantage of wealth, but the rich do not appreciate the advantage of wisdom."

38. Flattering lips are not an attribute of a believer, except in seeking wisdom.

39. The first step in the acquisition of wisdom is silence, the second listening, the third memory, the fourth practice, the fifth teaching others.

40. When you sit among the wise, be more eager to listen than to speak.

41. Whoever serves God honestly will be instructed in wisdom by Him, and the results will come from his heart to his tongue.

42. Nobody is wise unless he possesses three qualities: never to despise an inferior in learning who searches after wisdom, never to envy one who is more wealthy, and never to accept money for wisdom.

43. Ask the wise even foolish questions and reflect carefully on their answers.

44. The finest quality in man is to be an inquirer.

45. Whoever clothes himself in the garment of reticence to seek wisdom will wear the clothing of foolishness, therefore tear off the cloak of bashfulness when you seek wisdom.

46. Whoever increases in pride diminishes in wisdom.

47. The sage said: "I have found wisdom to be a mean between bashfulness and patience, but the fool stands between bashfulness and pride."

48. Hope perishes with dread, with bashfulness, and is ignorance.

49. When the believer loses wisdom he must seek it even from sceptics.

50. The sage exhorted his son: "Learn wisdom; for though thou wilt be an inferior to him who teaches thee, thou wilt be a superior to others."

51. How disgraceful is foolishness in an old man!

52. Teach wisdom to him who does not know it and learn

from him who knows. By doing this you will learn what you do not know and remember what you once knew.

53. The quest for wisdom in old age is like a mark made in the sand, but the quest of wisdom in youth is like an inscription on stone.

54. Do not deliver wisdom to one who is not fit to receive it, lest you wrong it; withhold it not from those who can appreciate it lest you wrong them. Requite not the wicked according to his wickedness lest you lose your own reward from God.

55. Obedience consists in performing what you are commanded to do and abstaining from what you are forbidden to do.

56. Poverty cannot disgrace the wise man, nor can lust enslave him.

57. When a fool contradicted a wise man, the latter retorted: "If you understood what I said you would not despise me; if I did not recognize what you say, I would condemn you. You, however, cannot appreciate what I said, therefore you condemned me; but I perceive your stupidity so I will judge you lightly."

58. A good idea without discussion is like a hidden treasure from which nothing is extracted.

59. There are two kinds of wisdom: the wisdom of the heart, which is the wisdom that profits a man; and the wisdom of the tongue, void of action, which brings man reproof from God.

60. There are four types among human beings: the man who knows and is aware that he knows—he is wise, so inquire of him; the man who knows, but is unaware that he knows—remind him and help him not to forget; the man who is ignorant and knows that he is ignorant—teach him; the man who is ignorant, but pretends to know—he is a fool, so keep away from him.

61. Say not of what you do not know "I know," lest you be suspected about what you *do* know.

62. There are no other virtues which have so beautiful a result as faith in God, honoring parents, love of wisdom and attentiveness to instruction.

63. When a fool does wrong, he blames others; it is a seeker of

instruction who blames himself; the wise and pious man blames neither himself nor others.

64. Be not ashamed to receive the truth from wherever it comes, even from an unattractive person.

65. One who acts the wise man without possessing wisdom is like an ass working the mill, going around and around without making progress.

66. Pity the respected man who has sunk low, the rich man who has become poor, and the wise man fallen among fools.

67. Nobody is more deserving of our sympathy than a wise man upon whom the judgment of a fool has fallen.

68. Cast no pearls before swine, for they can do nothing with them; deliver no wisdom to one who cannot appreciate its worth, for it is more precious than pearls, and he who does not seek it is worse than swine.

69. The reproof of a wise man who does not act according to his wisdom falls upon the heart like rain upon stone. He whose words do not accord with his actions puts himself to shame; therefore when the word issues from the tongue only, it does not penetrate the ear.

70. Nobody can detect the error of his teacher until he knows conflicting opinions.

71. The sage was asked, "How can it be becoming for an old man to learn?" He replied, "If ignorance is a disgrace to him, study must be becoming."

72. Four things an honorable man will not consider beneath his dignity: to stand up to greet his father, to pay deference to his guests, to inspect his own carriages even though he has a hundred servants, and to honor the wise man and share his wisdom.

73. Whoever sits among the wise is honored; whoever sits among fools is despised.

74. Beware of a fool who is devout and of a clever man who is a sinner.

75. The quest for wisdom is like a search for hidden treasure; gold and pearls cannot compare with it in value.

6

Man: Respecter of Limits

It is often claimed that Judaism is a religion of "this world" while Christianity and the Eastern religions are "other-worldly." To what extent this ignores the Jewish idea of immortality we shall examine in Chapter Nine. The assertion is, however, also a misreading of Judaism's view of what life is all about here and now.

The statement that Judaism exalts the pleasures and comforts of our bodies while other religions consider physical delights sinful is untrue; Judaism does permit and even encourages eating, drinking, sexuality, and the pleasures of worldly success. The heroes of the Hebrew Bible may be more human than Buddha or Jesus, if "human" means being married, having an occupation, living among people. Love of God means to the Jew loving one's parents, spouse, children, friends. But Moses and Jeremiah and Daniel can hardly be called worldlings. While the Hebrew Bible describes real people, it does not accept without question all that real people do. While it does not deny the pleasures of the human body, it does not make them the chief end of life. It achieves something infinitely more difficult: it sanctifies them. Sexuality is exalted by marriage, money-making by tithes, pleasure by the joy of doing commandments.

Post-Biblical Judaism is even more chastening. Partly under the influence of other philosophies, but largely because of the thrust of its own principles, rabbinic and medieval Judaism came to limit ever more sharply the uses and privileges of the instincts. Walking the narrow ridge between a mindless pursuit of pleasure, on the one hand, and a "spiritualized" Puritanism which denies pleasure, on the other, the sages tried to let man

be man, but in a sublimated and obedient way. Jews drink, but
first they say a blessing; alcohol is a means to sanctify Sabbath
and festival, not to escape life. Drugs are used for healing, not
for "kicks." The Rabbis made us temperate.

Hedonism and Puritanism are more alike than either would
admit. Both are obsessed with pleasure, and man is much more
than either sees. Judaism may well be the most pertinent alterna-
tive to the physical love-hate both philosophies display. Lust is
neither as noble as some assert nor as sinful as others pretend.
Eating and drinking and making love are good, but man is not
only animal, nor does God want only what man wants. A good
man will not easily turn from lawful pleasure, but neither will
he make it his chiefest joy.

How does a man learn to transcend his animal needs? How
does he do God's will while remaining a real person with a will
of his own? How may he link this world, which is real, with the
invisible Other World?

An eleventh-century philosopher whose work we include in
this chapter faces these questions without ambivalence. He was
no "worldling" so far as we know, but he was a sophisticated
European. Bahya ben Joseph ibn Pakuda was a rabbinic judge,
a preacher and mystical philosopher. His masterpiece *Hovot ha-
Levavot* (*The Duties of Hearts*)—a title which is itself a kind of
answer to our questions—was written in Spain in 1040. It is
about God and man, about what we can believe and what we
must do. Moving and thoughtful, it is perhaps the first great Jewish ethical or philosophic book. But it is much more: it tells men
about themselves and what they must reject in order to become
more than they have been. The chapter translated here deals
with abstinence. It asks: given what we need, what may we learn
to do without? What does God want us to enjoy and what to
renounce? What must we accept and what may we seek? His answers apply differently to different people. But nowhere does he
say: eat, drink and make love, for there is no tomorrow.

According to Bahya, Judaism is willing to let man be man,
but not on his own terms. It is a discipline, both resolutely re-

pressive and resolutely permissive. It makes this world desirable, or at least tolerable, by looking beyond itself. It makes man attractive, or at least bearable, by trying to bring him to God.

FROM

The Duties of Hearts
BY BAHYA IBN PAKUDA

What is abstinence?
Why do men require it in this world?

The word is ambiguous. Abstinence itself is a deep mystery. Only if its cover is removed and its seal broken can its nature be revealed and its purpose disclosed.

Abstinence can be defined, however, simply as controlling desire, that is, refraining from doing something we have the power and opportunity to do because we feel commanded to refrain. A person who abstains is someone who could act out, but does not. There are two reasons for controlling desire: one applies to every man, and even to many animals; the second is possible only for rational creatures who observe the Torah.

Abstinence in general is repression for the purpose of safeguarding our health and keeping our life in order. Without it we are like a country whose king rules according to one national pattern, or a doctor who gives the same medical prescription to the sick and well. Surely everyone who has any sense takes care of his health by occasionally repressing his desire for eating, drinking, sex, dress, conversation and other pleasurable activities. This kind of abstinence is taught by the Torah as well as by natural reason, and is for the improvement of our souls toward the world to come, as I shall explain later in this book, with God's help.

The need for abstinence in general is abundantly clear. God

created man in such a way as to discipline himself and test himself in this world so that he can become as pure as His angels, as
it is written: *If thou wilt walk in My ways and keep My charge
. . . I will give thee a place among the attending angels.* Intelligence requires corporeal bodies which only grow and thrive
on sustenance appropriate to themselves if they are ever to be
able to manage temptation.

God made men with a desire for the food they need in this
world; he gave men another urge which makes them desire sex
so that man reproduces himself; it was God who made eating
and sex pleasurable. He gave man an Evil Inclination that beck-
ons him to food, drink and sex and all the other gratifications
that make life possible, as Scripture said: *He set the world in
their heart . . . For every man to enjoy eating, drinking and
the rewards of his work is the gift of God.* But if man's Inclination masters his reason, it seduces him to excesses that injure his
soul and weaken his body. Accordingly, men require abstinence
from gratification in order to make their physical life orderly and
worthy of God's approval, as is indicated in the verse: *The man
who is kind and gives is good; he disposes of his affairs with
balance.*

Since men need to practice abstinence in order to improve
themselves in this world by taking from it only what they need,
it follows that there should be in our world some complete as-
cetics isolated from all the world's affairs from whom all the
rest of us may learn according to our own needs and character.
But the world would not be improved if everybody were ascetic,
for that would lead to abandoning civilization and producing no
new children. In fact, Scripture forbids this: *God did not create
the world to be empty; he formed it for men to live in.*

Abstinence is a cornerstone of the world; rational creatures
need to learn it as they need various other ideas and skills which
one or another nation contributes to the profit of men. Each
group takes what it needs and what is appropriate for itself. The
world would not be improved if everybody had the same ideas
or the same skills. Perfecting the world comes through combining

all the various contributions, as the sage said: "God makes everything beautiful in its own time"; and he said: "Everything has its
time."

We have expounded the general nature of abstinence and why
men need it to put their affairs in order in this world.

What is the definition of the special kind of abstinence that
religious Jews need? Our sages differ. Some say Jewish abstinence
is abandoning everything that alienates man from God. Some
say that it means despising the world and sharply curtailing our
needs. Some say it is peace of mind which precludes fantasies
that feed on idleness. Some say it is only faith in God, some that
it is dressing in the simplest possible clothing and eating only
what is necessary, despising any excess. Others say it means
abandoning love for all people in order to be alone with God.
Still others say it is gratitude for well-being and patience under
trial. Or that it means denying one's self all satisfactions and
gratifications except those our nature absolutely requires to survive.

This last definition is most nearly scriptural. We Jews need
such abstinence in order to let the reality principle rule over the
pleasure principle. For it is well-known that when desire controls
reason, all kinds of sin and delinquency are caused. People only
turn to the world when they abandon the Torah. Their Evil
Inclination seduces them into neglecting true civilization, which
could have been their salvation, and entices them to turn from
the way of their fathers which would have limited their indul-
gence to the bare necessities of life. To their children, power
seems pleasant, accumulation of wealth very precious, and position so desirable that they immerse themselves in status-seeking.
Their Evil Inclination makes them suffer the agony that comes
from the inevitability of frustrated desire. The world rules them,
stops their ears and blinds their eyes. None of them works at
anything but his own pleasure when he has even an outside
chance to achieve it. Pleasure is his real Torah and his religion,
so that pleasure-seeking finally separates him from God. As the

Bible says: *Your own evil shall correct you and your failures reprove you. For it is evil and bitter that you have left the Lord, your God, and have no fear of Me.*

Other people have been denied such gratification, but keep thinking of it and yearn for it night and day, as is said: "He contemplates evil on his bed and sets out on a way not good." Both groups are immersed in pleasure-seeeking and yet are exhausted too soon to get much out of their search. They fail in business, their personalities shrink, and their choices always turn out wrong. They make foolish estimates of what is more and less worthwhile, as is said: "They changed their glory to imitate an ox."

These people are ruled by overpowering and habitual arrogance. They have invested in a bankrupt business which can only ruin them and make them brood over their vicissitudes. The more they get involved, the further away from reality they grow. Their attachment to their Evil Inclination brings darkness as thick as smoke around them. The more the world grows in their heart the more attractive it seems. They work tirelessly for it, while wrecking their own minds. The more truly civilized the world becomes, the more threatened are their rationalizations, until each comes to think his evil way the best and takes his wandering as walking the straight path. They make their whims a law and a system of morality.

Fathers bequeath it to their children; teachers indoctrinate it; rulers command their communities to follow it, and authorities are zealous to fix the Evil Inclination as an authority among their people.

Thus the peculiar becomes familiar and the right way strange. Whoever is satisfied even with plenty seems over-abstinent and ungrateful for not doing what he sees his neighbor do. A person who works only for what he actually needs is called lazy, and one who neglects to increase his holdings is called a loser. A man who considers enough enough is thought impotent, and only one who succeeds in business is a go-getter. Neighbors honor only the successful man; they make him their leader, form groups for his sake, attack those outside their group and flatter those within their circle.

Men make their bellies their gods; their clothing is their Torah; their ethics is improving their own neighborhood. They make incredibly ridiculous mistakes which end in boredom. Oppressed by their sexual urges, they seek the reward which is due obedient servants for their sins and the title of saint for practicing their evil customs, as our sages predicted: "They sin like Zimri and expect Phineas' reward." *

Since the Evil Inclination has overcome even the most religious Jews, we must take a stand against it and on behalf of the special kind of abstinence we have described.

In renunciation we withstand the Evil Inclination and bring those who have erred back to religion, thus improving both our faith and the world. We need religious Jews who will accept the responsibility for a special abstinence in order to influence others who impulsively seek only sexual gratification. We need physicians of the soul to bring healing to persons whose Evil Inclinations have mastered their reason and who have been seduced from their religious duties by absorption in luxuries. Abstinent teachers will try to cure those whose faith is sick or who are suffering from ambivalence or who are running away from serving God. They will bring them back to obedience with promises of God's forgiveness. If someone comes to them who has forgotten God, they will remind him. They will beatify the saint, love the lover of God, and make much of any man who makes much of God. If someone sins, they will urge him to turn in repentance immediately. If someone is sick, they will visit him, bringing with them whatever they own and do not absolutely need. They will help anyone in trouble. Like the sun, they will illuminate both those above and those below themselves.

These few of whom I write are the secret saviors of the world like the fifty men for whose sake even the city of Sodom could

* Phineas' family was named to the priesthood after his zeal in killing Zimri, who had brought a Midianite woman into the Israelite camp in the wilderness and had intercourse with her.

have been saved. Of their immortality the proverb says: "The fruit of the righteous is a tree of life." And Deborah said: "Those who love God shall be like the sun in his might." Their precious kind of abstinence was actually practiced by prophets and the pious in every generation, as they themselves wrote.

7

Man: The Penitent

Recent experiments at the University of Chicago have provided documentation for an old Jewish truth: learning how to be good is a kind of learning; the intellectual and the moral are intimately related. Children learn to be ethical in a way not dissimilar from the way they learn anything else. While moralizing and exemplifying have only limited value, opening the minds of the young to thinking pertinently about what is right and wrong can be useful, provided the thinking is not too abstract or complicated.

This view was propounded with vigor by Rabbi Israel Lipkin in the nineteenth century. In the East European town of Salant, where he studied, he was familiarly called the Salanter. He created, almost single-handed, the *Musar* or Morality Movement in traditionalist European Judaism. For him the fruits of study were good deeds, and the road to goodness was study and practice. Eschewing the emotionalism and anti-intellectualism of Hasidism, he insisted that mind alone was not enough. Decency and human compassion were the touchstone of Jewish accomplishment. He insisted upon fair-dealing with all men and with all governments, even the Russian at its most inhumanly cruel. He stressed not only ritual piety, but fair business practices and avoidance of slander. He taught the values of physical work and persistent morality. His influence has been called the most pervasive and significant in nineteenth-century Judaism.

But for us the *Musar* movement and, especially, Rabbi Israel's *Letter on Ethics* raises problems. We know of many "wise" men who are not good. Great scientists in Germany created laboratories of extermination. Learned Jews have often locked themselves within the ghetto of scholarship, never to be heard of again, while their world went up in flames. Reading and studying do not always make better or kinder men no more than do ritual piety or the Kantian will-to-be-good.

Rabbi Israel Salanter was aware of these problems. Because he feared an arid kind of learning that hermetically sealed Judaism, he created a movement that tried to break the seal and open up thought to the world of real people with real ethical tasks. Because emotionalism untrained by thought was suspect to him, he linked doing with knowing. Because he knew how hard it is to turn from evil to good, he wrote the *Letter on Ethics*, which follows. He deeply feared the divine wrath that could hurl the wicked man into darkness. Because he loved men and knew their weakness, he struggled to lift them to nobler aspiration and more just lives.

With some of his conclusions we may no longer agree. It is difficult for us to imagine Jews who sincerely thought keeping kosher was more obviously God's will than keeping honest books. It is difficult for us to concede that reading books about punishment for gossip will keep men from gossiping. It is difficult to believe that a fear of the effects of our sins can keep us from committing such sins.

Rabbi Salanter asks whether the inclination to do wrong is simple passion or demonic Other Nature. He examines both kinds of existing human temperaments, but concedes permanent victory to neither. Man is harried and confused, but free. If his sins are deep and difficult to extirpate, they are nonetheless not quite ineluctable. They can still be rooted out of his life. But how?

Perhaps by thinking about them and about God. Not thinking philosophically, but thinking in a way connected with the realities of our lives. Not by rationalizing and saying: "we're only human," but by using our reason to penetrate and excise our rebelliousness. By using reason we may yet see ourselves in all our human uniqueness, not as saints but as creatures with special temptations and yet with a special ability to resist such temptations. For if sin is regression, childishness or fundamental immaturity, goodness can still become a habit.

Like Aristotle among the Greeks, Salanter asks why man should not habituate himself to goodness. For him the ethical is a skill, a style, a way of life. It can be chosen, learned, practiced, achieved. One must begin with his weakest sin and, by uncovering it, control its power to persuade. The therapy of taking action against our failings will annihilate any ambivalence which "hardens" or paralyzes our heart. The regimen of Jewish practice can conduce to goodness.

Not automatically, of course. Salanter has no easy road to salvation or grace. But, with patience, the Jew can learn to turn, can acquire the mature man's genius of continually making his way back to what he ought to be becoming. By doing what his body lets him do, his soul is freed to achieve the miracle of spontaneity. By trying hard to do good where trying still helps, the Jew can be helped to become a naturally good person. By helping others to turn, he finds himself turned around to God and once again capable of attaining the self he knows himself created to be.

FROM

Letter on Ethics

BY ISRAEL SALANTER

Man is free to fantasy, but is bound by his reason. His fantasy leads him headlong on pleasure's path, never fearing the inevitable future, the time when God will punish all his evil deeds severely. No one else will be punished for him; he alone will reap the fruit of his sin. The man who sins is the one who is punished. All the same it is very hard for a person to say: this is my

own fault and I am afraid. The hurts of this world are trivial
compared to punishment for sins. Man will suffer as much in a
day then as he could now in a year.

Our fantasy is the evil enemy within. Yet we have the power
to resist it by attending to the truth of reason, by considering
what sin costs us compared to what it offers. Fantasy is an on-
rushing stream in which reason drowns unless it is put safely
aboard ship. A person's emotions are like a storm in his spirit.

To know how we are to proceed, let us first remember that in
such matters there is always a general principle and concrete,
specific examples. Without a general principle, there can be no
particulars which exemplify it. But there can be a general class
with no individual members. First importance attaches to a general principle from which a number of particulars follow.

Let us then consider what religious service we owe God, what
general rule concerning it might lead to particular conclusions as
to how we should live.

We recognize immediately as a principle of faith that God is
our Judge who gives each man the fruit of his deeds. If a man's
life is evil he will be badly punished here and now or in the
world-to-come. Man cannot know how much or what kind of
punishment awaits him. But if his work is pure and straight-
forward, he will be blessed in this world with noble pleasure and
with even more in that Eden which is far beyond the power of
human intellect or emotion to comprehend. Knowing this is our
first step toward the service of God.

Our sages have said: Habbakuk summarized all the Torah in
one verse: *The righteous shall live by his faith.* And in the Talmud they say: Men who would control their fantasy should consider the hardship in performing a *mitzvah* against the profit
and the pleasure of a sin against its cost.

Still, bitterness and suffering repress this principle in us; it is
hidden in our mind's depths and never becomes visible unless we
plant the soil of our hearts with ethical seeds. That is why our
general principle alone is barren and does not bind our bodies in
the discipline of religion. That too is why from this general prin-

ciple alone no specifics follow which could guard us from sins that tempt us. So we are always falling into enormous sins: sins of the tongue that our spirits cannot control, dishonest business practices and, especially, neglect of the study of Torah.

Generally speaking, we are all sick. As the Talmud evaluates people: the greater the man, the greater his Evil Inclination. We all fall into enormous sins which do not seem large to us because our hearts are dark. If we look through a telescope, we understand finally that what seems small to us may be very large, though the stars are infinitely larger than they seem through our telescope. The Torah explains with perfect logic that sins are very attractive and very powerful.

This conclusion is evidenced by a passage in the Talmud: the First Temple was destroyed because of idolatry, lewdness, and murder. But the people of the Second Temple studied the Torah, observed its precepts and did good deeds. Why, then, was it destroyed? Because of senseless hate. In the First Temple, public sin was punished with an exile whose end was public. The later generation whose sin was not public suffered a mysterious fate. The gross iniquity of the First Temple was perfectly clear. But the sins of the later ones, which could only be perceived after sharp scrutiny, proved to be far more grave because more subtle and consequential.

The Rabbis asked: Who was greater, the earlier generation or the later? And their answer was: The Temple was restored to the former generations, but not to the later. The later generation, greater in good deeds and in study of Torah, were, as we suggested earlier, though greater men, also greater sinners. A wise man knows that the sins of great men lead to profound evil.

Now, despite human evasions, the unknown day of one's death will come suddenly and God will call man to account for everything he did all his life. Nothing will be ignored. More bitter than death will be that end from which none escapes and from which there is no refuge. Thus the Bible says: *There is hope only for the living. It is better to be a living dog than a dead lion.* The Rabbis interpret this verse to mean that while a man is

alive he still has hope of turning, but when he dies, it is all over
for him.

Therefore, while we still live, let us hurry to improve our ways.
The road is full of stumbling-blocks, but we need not fear the
day of our death even if it is right in front of us and we remember what it is. In the Talmud it is said: Even if our own eyes
witness the death of other men just like us, that by itself does
not give us the power to turn wholeheartedly to our Creator
before whom we, too, must come for final judgment and who
will prosecute all our evil deeds. The other side of the coin is
the Biblical verse: *It is better to go to the house of mourning
than to the house of feasting, for that is the end of all men, and
the living will put it upon his heart.*

It is the banality of our sins which has numbed our heart and
made it stone, as our sages say in the Talmud: When a man sins
repeatedly, he foolishly thinks sins are permitted; these are
the sins which will surround us on Judgment Day, as our sages
said: The sins on which man tramples will someday surround
him. Have we no hope? Is there no healing?

Let us try to understand the nature of sin. We have seen that
there are two kinds: one flows from unbridled lust which covets
what is momentarily pleasant without looking to the future, however bitter that may ultimately be. An example of this type is
immoral business practices. The foolish or immature man loves
to eat what tastes good, forgetting that overeating leads to grave
distress. Therefore, our teachers said: Who is wise? The man who
foresees future consequences. The same idea is expressed else-
where in the Talmud: No man sins unless he is possessed by a
foolish spirit.

The whole task of man in the service of God is to think hard
about the fear of God and the terror of His punishment, as
described in ethical books, *aggadot* and *Midrashim.** With his
ears he will almost hear and with his own eyes almost see the
scope and nature of punishment as our Rabbis said in the Talmud: Let a judge (or, indeed, any man) always imagine a drawn

---

* The various rabbinic sermonic commentaries on the Bible.

sword over his body and *Gehinnom* (hell) open below him. If a man can imagine that, he will come to understand, turn and be healed.

Great is the evil of man on earth. Nobody seeks justice. None understands the fear of God. They therefore sin in not setting aside fixed times to cultivate that kind of fear which draws understanding from the faith hidden in the secret recesses of the heart, in order to broaden it, uphold it, and give it strength and authority to rule their bodies in accordance with the Torah.

We do not find this kind of sin exemplified in worldly life, since any man in trouble thinks about ways of escaping it. Lust, however, is never the cause of sins of omission, amazingly enough. Passion does not prevent meditation on the fear of God and His correction. Sins of omission do not fall into the class of sins caused by lust, but are rather a consequence of man's unclean spirit. Many sins are not even pleasurable.

This explains the two conflicting opinions about the Evil Inclination and the Good Inclination. One school of thought, the better known, considers the Evil Inclination to be the power of uncleanness in man which tempts him to sin, and the Good Inclination the power of holiness in man which encourages him to all kinds of good. To this school of thought belong most of our greatest teachers.

The second school holds that the Evil Inclination is the power of man's lust which looks passionately for the momentary pleasure it cherishes and adores, while the Good Inclination is straight thinking which looks to the future. It is the fear of God and God's terrible judgment which makes man choose the ethical, suppressing his lust so as ultimately to reach the highest pleasure, indescribable glory.

We see that men sin differently. One chooses to sin by neglecting Torah rather than by dishonest business practice or by not giving charity—another just the opposite. This is true of all sins: no one sins just like anyone else. If the Evil Inclination were only the power of uncleanness which tempts man, why would it not seduce all men in the same way? But if we admit that the

Evil Inclination is the force of a man's own lust, then we know why: a man's lust is bound up with his specific temperament, birth, age and concerns. Since men are different, so are their sins.

But this does not fit the facts precisely. Do we not see with our own eyes people who are unmoved by lust committing terrible sins? Sometimes their self-interest even opposes them, as, for instance, the man who longs for illusory honor while looking down on the authentic honor he could get from obedience to God. It must be the spirit of uncleanness that mixes him up and makes him do evil against his own vain desire.

Both schools of thought are partly correct. The Evil Inclination is *both* lust and the spirit of uncleanness. The Good Inclination is straight thinking (uncorrupted by sin and lust) and sees the consequences of our act, and it is also the holy spirit in man. For man has two aspects: physical and spiritual.

Man is created body and soul, a visible body and a soul inferred from the acts of the body. Human strategies to keep man's soul in his body serve the needs only of his body, strengthening it with wholesome food and protecting it against danger. That is the way man guards his soul while it is within his body. There is no natural protection for the soul, however, for no one sees or feels it. How can we save our souls?

We can serve God. We can strengthen the Good Inclination, the power of holiness and straight thinking. We can repress the Evil Inclination, including both the power of uncleanness and lust. From the physical side this means feeding the Evil Inclination with "good food": meditation, fear of God, and ethical direction from the pure Torah. In the story of Job, say our teachers, Job is accused of abolishing the fear of God by blaming God for everything that happens, including sin. God created the Evil Inclination, says the Talmud, but he also created the Torah as an antidote. They teach us that Torah's antidote to sin is the fear of God it produces, which, they claim, Job tried to eliminate.

Even physically, men's psychological ills improve if man sets his mind on fearing God, as the Torah teaches. It is important for us to know precisely that every sin has its severe punishment and every good deed its great and marvelous reward. Each sin must be considered separately: pride in connection with the portion of Torah that relates to pride, business ethics with the relevant part of the Torah, and so on for each sin and each commandment in the Torah.

The essential healing power of Torah for ills caused by the Evil Inclination comes from hard study and deep meditation on specific, relevant laws. For we see that men naturally avoid many sins if it is hard for them to commit them at the time. Yet there are far graver sins which men commit lightly. For example, most Jews, indeed almost all of us, wash before we eat even if we are famished. Yet the same Jews gossip freely for no profound reason, and gossip is much worse than not washing before meals.

The best way to keep away from sin is to make it a habit not to sin. If a man tries to behave decently, for example, to avoid gossip with all his power, he still finds it harder than eating without washing, until his habit becomes second nature. And that is true of all kinds of sins, depending on the person, the time and the place. All places are not the same. In each place some sins are more easily avoided than others because of the customs of the place which make them look repulsive. It is well known that human nature can be changed only by study and habituation. Therefore, the essential task is to prepare oneself to keep from a sin or to do a good deed by hard study of the law which pertains to that sin or that good deed. It is especially important that the study be precise for the person to acquire a natural revulsion toward that sin. For example, in our country the prohibition against non-kosher food is so natural to Jewish people that it takes no effort not to eat it; it simply seems repulsive. Every butcher who had doubts about whether some meat was kosher would ask a rabbi, even if it might cost him money. Fear of God has become natural and habitual, and he could not allow himself to make another Jew sin with non-kosher food.

In business matters, however, the situation is very different. Most men will not on their own initiative examine the possibility that they have been dishonest until someone else accuses them. Even then they formulate evasive responses. But in the Torah all commandments are equally binding. *You must not eat non-kosher food* is no more a law than *You must not exploit your neighbor nor rob him.* Though most Jews are physically unable to eat non-kosher food, still in business matters even learned men violate the law against exploiting our neighbor, a sin so grave that neither the Day of Atonement nor even death atones for it.

But even if a man sets his mind on studying the laws that relate to money matters as best he can, and especially if his central aim is to learn how to avoid theft and dishonesty, his lust and the general business atmosphere would militate against easy success. It is hard to become convinced that honesty in business is as obligatory as the dietary laws. If a man is tempted to commit even an unusual kind of sin like adultery, which our sages considered a rare and irrational exception, he should meditate on the fear of God and ethics in the rabbinic sources, and in particular he should study thoroughly the laws of sexuality to obey them.

One should begin where the Evil Inclination is weakest. Thus, in the Talmud we hear of a lustful sinner who kept leaven over the *Pesah* holiday, but reduced his sin by changing it for bread belonging to a non-Jew. Should we not be frightened and chastened before the example of earlier generations of Jews when even such a sinner had a natural tendency to reduce his sin? In our own time we are proud and defiant sinners. Even where habit leads us constantly astray, we do not set our minds to reducing its attractiveness nor to lessening the scope of our disobedience. Our evil is as great as that of a defiant apostate.

The essential remedy for our condition is to reflect in fear that a sin committed in defiance of God is infinitely worse than one committed for our own pleasure. We can bring terrible punishment upon our souls without even any gratification of our lust. Another crucial remedy is to study the laws as well as we can; that requires leisure, personal concern and care. The fruit of our study will slowly but surely give us the strength to resist damnation, or at least to sin without downright defiance. Ultimately, study of the law can enable us to transform our natures so that we would no longer consider sinning, even when it is hard for us not to.

There is another way to handle the Evil Inclination, though human intelligence and sense perception cannot see what makes it work. I mean the way described in the Talmud: study of Torah saves a man from sin. The passage studied may not relate to any specific sin. Yet study as such prevents sins like gossip, for the spirituality of Torah is a protection against all kinds of wickedness.

All our strategies to heal the Evil Inclination are physical, even meditation on the fear of God and study of the laws. For the final spiritual cure only comes spontaneously and accidentally since the commandment to study Torah is part of a larger whole. A Jew studies to regulate his entire life before God and man, however strong his Evil Inclination may be. We must always study, in order to fulfill our obligation, even if our Evil Inclination rarely masters us. If we study more than we are required to, our Evil Inclination seems to be tamed, somehow or other.

The physical remedy is meditation on the fear of God and study of the law which apparently cures. But a man must use it properly. Just as in disease a cure is quantitatively and qualitatively relative to the illness, so with spiritual sickness the cure is proportional to the disease. As much as his Evil Inclination masters him, so much should a man increase his meditation on the fear of God and his study of the law. If he does not, the general spiritual force of Torah to heal will never empower him to conquer his Evil Inclination. Spiritual success depends on quite mundane work. For the enemy who lies in wait for man is our Evil Inclination, ever trying to make our heart a stone so that we will no longer feel our deep sin nor see our failings. Ultimately, such a man will not be able to save himself by meditating on the fear of God or even to seek for a cure.

A man should, therefore, set his mind to help others to meditation, awe and ethical instruction. Since it is easier to see the sins of others and how they need instruction, one must try harder to improve himself. In that way he will inspire many others, increase the fear of God and the improvement of many men. Slowly the study of ethics will lead one to right action and to a cure both physical and spiritual. For anyone who helps others will commit no sin, as the Talmud puts it.

It is very important to learn to lead others ethically in order to save them from damnation. If one is compassionate toward other men, God will be compassionate toward him. There is no greater love than to rouse men to fear, for then they will see for themselves how great is their danger and, fearing for their future, they will turn to God, depart from evil and do as much good as they can. Any man who awakens others to good has a share in all that will come, a paradise which no eye has ever seen. Human reason cannot grasp how much good flows from how small a beginning.

The effort is small. The reward can be great. Its value is immeasurable. Every man should devote the powers of his mind and body to this great task—if, indeed, he is a man with a soul.

8

Man: The Sufferer

Many men seem to be religious because they feel deeply the problem of evil. If there is no God, the problem of suffering is no problem; but if there is a God, it is the most agonizing of questions. Why should an innocent child die of leukemia while a tyrant lives to a ripe old age? Why are six million Jews killed in death camps while their enemies continue to prosper? Why are men like John F. Kennedy and Mohandas Gandhi assassinated while their moral inferiors continue to live on in peace? Even if we ourselves learn to tame our Evil Inclination and live by the Torah, why are our lives so often shadowed by suffering or death? Though the Bible promises man blessing for obedience, he often appears cursed by life.

The crucial question is how God can be both omnipotent and good. But there is also a most difficult question about man. If the righteous suffer, why be righteous? If nature is deaf to human cries and blind to human values, as great thinkers from Epicurus to Sartre have thought, then how is it possible for man even to be, let alone to be good? Life itself, not just the struggle for morality, is called into question.

If we are met with cosmic indifference, why should we, too, not be indifferent to the value of life? That question has tormented the best minds of our generation. No wonder Albert Camus called it the one real philosophical issue. When we stand at the grave of our own child, it is difficult to be sentimental about the dignity of man. In autonomous human bitterness, we demand with Job that God answer: "Why?"

To this angry question, as to so many others, Rav Saadyah Gaon, the eminent leader of tenth-century Babylonian Jewry and head of its rabbinic academy, addressed himself. In one of the earliest and still most important masterpieces of Jewish philosophy, *Emunot ve-Deot (Beliefs and Opinions)*, Saadyah defends Judaism against its heretics within and its enemies without. Along with other important issues of his day, Saadyah attacks the problem of the suffering of the righteous. What he really cares about is the nature and transformation of man. Can man become human without suffering? Can he avoid the damnation which is emptiness if God fails to show him the awesome reality of human existence? If sinners flourish, that may turn out to be their most terrible suffering; if the righteous feel pain, that may be their highest privilege. His theory comes perilously close to masochism, but, looking back on our own lives, we know that it also seems to be true.

Saadyah argues that man's ability to undergo trial is the consequence and evidence of his pre-eminence in God's world. He has no doubt that our world is the center of the universe and our self the center of the world. Man's superiority, like his suffering, is not the work of his own hands, however, but of God's unmerited grace. Man only seems small to us because we see the God in whose image he is made as tiny or remote. But for Saadyah, God's power and wisdom are both scientifically demonstrable. The Bible is not only correct; it is self-evident. God made everything and put it into man's hand. He also gave man the freedom to destroy it, or to improve it under God. That freedom is the root of all our suffering, for we sin and in sinning bring pain on ourselves. This world is man's kindergarten; he can learn only by trying. When he fails, he suffers; but that is how he becomes a man. In this world, therefore, even suffering makes man more human; only in the next will he need no pain. But the decisive choice of Everlasting Reward is also man's to make. His choices have cosmic consequence.

Still, the question haunts us: could God not have designed a world that bypassed Auschwitz? If pain is necessary, is it not also too destructive? Sin may, indeed, require punishment, but what sin could require the death of millions of children? Saadyah's answer turns out to be pious rather than philosophic. Perhaps our own unanswered and unanswerable questions come from weaker faith rather than greater suffering.

Perhaps our responses are intellectual rather than religious. If our world often seems to us worse than Saadyah's did to him, the next world seems too remote to offer us adequate reparation. We want answers here and cannot find them. We are uneasy about waiting for the next world's rewards because we do not trust Saadyah's God.

FROM

Beliefs and Opinions

BY SAADYAH GAON

Even though we see that there are many creatures in the world we need not be perplexed as to what they signify. There is an objective natural standard by which we can determine which one is ultimate. When we examine this standard, we find that the purpose of all creation is man.

Both custom and logic put the most important in the center of the less important. Beginning with the smallest things, the kernel is in the center of leaves because it is the most important part of a plant whose very life depends on it. If the seed of a tree is edible, it is found in the center of the fruit, like a nut. If it is inedible, the kernel is still the center of the fruit and is protected by an edible core. Similarly, the yolk of an egg is in the center because the chicken develops only from it. And so, the heart of man is in the middle of his chest, because it is the seat of man's intellectual and physical power. And the instrument of sight is in the middle of the eye.

When we see that most things are like this and then find the earth is in the middle of the heavens with planets circling around it on all sides, we conclude that the purpose of the whole universe must be found on earth. Both earth itself and water are inanimate; animals cannot speak; only man is left. Therefore, necessarily, he is the purpose of all creation.

In Scripture we find the Creator saying: *I have made the earth and created man upon it.* Even the beginning of the Torah enumerates all creatures. When He had made them all, God says, *Let us make man,* like one who first builds a palace, furnishes it and improves it, and afterwards brings in its true owner.

Our God has informed us through His prophets that He made man superior to all His other creatures, when He said: *Rule over the fish of the sea and the fowl of the air.* Or as the Psalm has it: Adonai, *our Lord, how excellent is Your name in all the earth!* This is so because He gave man the power to serve Him when He set before him the power of choice, commanding him to choose the good, as He said: *See, I have set before you this day life and good, death and evil . . . Therefore, choose life!* To lend weight to this passage God worked miracles and wonders so that we would believe it.

When we investigated scientifically what gives man his superiority, we discovered it to be the wisdom which God gave him and taught him, as it is said: *He teaches man knowing.* With wisdom man preserves the past and sees the future, and subdues animals so that they work the earth for him and bring him its product. With wisdom he brings water from the earth's depths so that it flows on the surface. He can even make wheels which water the soil automatically. With wisdom he builds magnificent houses, wears the finest clothing and prepares the tastiest foods. With wisdom, he succeeds in commanding armies and conducting governments whose authority other men accept. With wisdom he attains the knowledge of astronomy. If anyone should believe that a creature exists superior to man, he would have to show its qualities, or at least some of them. He will never find such a creature.

If that is so, it is only right that man be commanded, warned, rewarded and punished, since he is the hub of the universe and its foundation, as the Bible says: *For the pillars of the earth are God's, and He has set the world upon them.* And it says: *The righteous man is the foundation of the universe.* When I considered these fundamental truths and what follows from them, I understood that the belief in man's superiority is not a mere fantasy of our minds nor a prejudice of our prideful hearts, but simple truth. The wise God made us superior only to hear His commandments and prohibitions, as Scripture says: *He said to man, "Behold the fear of the Lord is wisdom; to depart from evil is understanding."*

I pondered how the whole universe depends on man whose body is small and unattractive. I mulled over this and found that, even though his body is small, his mind is broader than heaven and earth, since his knowledge includes everything in all of them and he comes to know even what is above them by whom they exist, the Creator God. Scripture has it: *Your works are wonderful, and my soul knows it well.*

I reflected on man's mortality and it became clear to me that the Creator gave him a short life only in this world, the world of care. But we are also promised an eternal life after we are transmuted, as Scripture says: *He asked life from You and You gave it to him, length of days forever and ever.*

Why is man's superiority built on a weak body comprised of blood and phlegm and the two galls, and not of pure and immortal parts? To want such a condition would be to want man to be a celestial or an angel. For the human body is the purest of earthly mixtures. Anything still purer would have to be celestial or angelic. Whoever would prefer a human body composed of elements other than those that actually form it is really asking to destroy men, as one who wants heaven to be entirely dust or earth all fire asks the absurd and opposes God's wisdom. The Bible says: *How great are Your works, O Lord! In wisdom You made them all.*

I further thought about the illnesses that come upon man, and I thought: "If only he could be delivered or protected from them." But then I found these illnesses to be good for him, because when he is sick he may turn from his sins and humble himself before his God. Illnesses improve the human condition in the view of Scripture: *He is improved by pain upon his bed.*

I thought about how heat and cold control man, how he is in danger of the poison of reptiles and carnivorous animals. But these, too, can improve him, for if he felt no pain he would fear no divine punishment. If God said to him, "I shall punish you painfully," he would not even know what the words meant. So God made him suffer all these troubles in order to recognize what might be, as Scripture says of the great heat: *For a day shall come burning like a furnace.* And it compares punishment to a serpent: *Their wine is serpent's venom.*

Many human passions lead to evil. The wise God gave us desires only to put evil to its proper use, with the help of reason which He mercifully gave us, too. The desire for food is to sustain our body; sexual passion sustains our species. Each appetite must be examined to see what is appropriate to it. If man exercises his desire in a permissible way he is praiseworthy; if he misuses it he is reprehensible, as the Bible says: *The desire of righteous men is only good, but the hope of the wicked leads to wrath.* And it says: *Only the wicked man boasts of his passion.*

I wondered why God prepared the awful and eternal agony of fire. I saw that besides torment God offered us the eternal delight of everlasting reward. If there were not these two alternatives, nothing would make man hope profoundly or fear profoundly, as it is said: *These to life eternal, and those to reproaches and everlasting abhorrence.*

I meditated that a guilty man must, according to Jewish law, be executed in this world by one of the four means of capital punishment. Clearly, this too is for his benefit and is not irrational. For reason dictates that a poisoned or diseased limb must be amputated in order to save a person's life. So the species must kill one of its members who has been corrupted and is corrupting his world so that the rest of the species might be saved. Scripture declares: *Those who remain will hear of it and be afraid.*

After discussing the categories of God's just ordinance for men, I only add that, whatever a believer may worry about, he need only think hard about the problem and doubtless will discover a reason in Divine Wisdom, as Scripture says: *All the paths of God are loving and true.*

The most agonizing test of theodicy not only in Jewish history but in human history, not only in our time but in any time, was Auschwitz. The camps, the murder of six million Jews, radically changes all our sentimental thinking about God's goodness and man's dignity. If there is a God, how could there ever have been an Auschwitz?

Elie Wiesel came to Auschwitz young, hardly more than a boy. He left broken, impassioned, and has since become a decisively significant Jewish writer. He cannot forget what he saw though he sometimes cannot believe it any more himself. He will not allow us to forget though we can hardly bear the memory of the terror. And we were not even there! Wiesel will remain permanently in the literature of Israel as a sign and a task: the sign of the greatest catastrophe in man's history and the task to remember the awful glory of those death camps in which not only men but God was seen to die.

FROM

Night

BY ELIE WIESEL

The summer was coming to an end. The Jewish year was nearly over.

On the eve of Rosh Hashanah, the last day of that accursed year, the whole camp was electric with the tension which was in all our hearts. In spite of everything, this day was different from

any other. The last day of the year. The word "last" rang very
strangely. What if it were indeed the last day?

They gave us our evening meal, a very thick soup, but no one
touched it. We wanted to wait until after prayers. At the place
of assembly, surrounded by the electrified barbed wire, thousands
of silent Jews gathered, their faces stricken.

Night was falling. Other prisoners continued to crowd in, from
every block, able suddenly to conquer time and space and submit both to their will.

"What are You, my God," I thought angrily, "compared to this
afflicted crowd, proclaiming to You their faith, their anger, their
revolt? What does Your greatness mean, Lord of the Universe,
in the face of all this weakness, this decomposition, and this
decay? Why do You still trouble their sick minds, their crippled
bodies?"

Ten thousand men had come to attend the solemn service,
heads of the blocks, Kapos, functionaries of death.

"Bless the Eternal. . ."

The voice of the officiant had just made itself heard. I thought
at first it was the wind.

"Blessed be the Name of the Eternal!"

Thousands of voices repeated the benediction; thousands of
men prostrated themselves like trees before a tempest.

"Blessed be the Name of the Eternal!"

Why, but why should I bless Him? In every fiber I rebelled.
Because He had had thousands of children burned in His pits?
Because He kept six crematories working night and day, on Sun-
days and feast days? Because in His great might He had created
Auschwitz, Birkenau, Buna and so many factories of death? How
could I say to Him: "Blessed art Thou, Eternal, Master of the
Universe, who chose us from among the races to be tortured day
and night, to see our fathers, our mothers, our brothers, end in
the crematory? Praised be Thy holy Name, Thou who hast
chosen us to be butchered on Thine altar?"

I heard the voice of the officiant rising up, powerful yet at the same time broken, amid the tears, the sobs, the sighs of the whole congregation:

"All the earth and the universe are God's!"

He kept stopping every moment, as though he did not have the strength to find the meaning beneath the words. The melody choked in his throat.

And I, mystic that I had been, I thought:

"Yes, man is very strong, greater than God. When You were deceived by Adam and Eve, You drove them out of Paradise. When Noah's generation displeased You, You brought down the Flood. When Sodom no longer found favor in Your eyes, You made the sky rain down fire and sulphur. But these men here, whom You have betrayed, whom You have allowed to be tortured, butchered, gassed, burned, what do they do? They pray before You! They praise Your Name!"

"All creation bears witness to the greatness of God!"

Once, New Year's Day had dominated my life. I knew that my sins grieved the Eternal; I implored his forgiveness. Once, I had believed profoundly that upon one solitary deed of mine, one solitary prayer, depended the salvation of the world.

This day I had ceased to plead. I was no longer capable of lamentation. On the contrary, I felt very strong. I was the accuser, God the accused. My eyes were open and I was alone—terribly alone in a world without God and without man. Without love or mercy. I had ceased to be anything but ashes, yet I felt myself to be stronger than the Almighty, to whom my life had been tied for so long. I stood amid that praying congregation, observing it like a stranger.

The service ended with the Kaddish. Everyone recited the Kaddish over his parents, over his children, over his brothers, and over himself.

We stayed for a long time at the assembly place. No one dared to drag himself away from this mirage. Then it was time to go to bed and slowly the prisoners made their way over to their blocks. I heard people wishing one another a Happy New Year!

I ran off to look for my father. And at the same time I was afraid of having to wish him a Happy New Year when I no longer believed in it.

He was standing near the wall, bowed down, his shoulders sagging as though beneath a heavy burden. I went up to him, took his hand and kissed it. A tear fell upon it. Whose was that tear? Mine? His? I said nothing. Nor did he. We had never understood one another so clearly.

The sound of the bell jolted us back to reality. We had to go to bed. We came back from far away. I raised my eyes to look at my father's face leaning over mine, to try to discover a smile or something resembling one upon the aged, dried-up countenance. Nothing. Not the shadow of an expression. Beaten.

Yom Kippur. The Day of Atonement.

Should we fast? The question was hotly debated. To fast would mean a surer, swifter death. We fasted here the whole year round. The whole year was Yom Kippur. But others said that we should fast simply because it was dangerous to do so. We should show God that even here, in this enclosed hell, we were capable of singing His praises.

I did not fast, mainly to please my father, who had forbidden me to do so. But further, there was no longer any reason why I should fast. I no longer accepted God's silence. As I swallowed my bowl of soup, I saw in the gesture an act of rebellion and protest against Him.

And I nibbled my crust of bread.

In the depths of my heart, I felt a great void.

9

Man: Mortal and Immortal

Heidegger, the modern philosopher, and Hemingway, the novelist, who are not alike in any other way, both consider death the decisive fact of man's life. Psychologists describe much of what we do and leave undone as a mask for death, a denial of the inevitable. And modern funeral practices have come under serious criticism as neo-pagan evasions of the fact of death. Sex was once the unspeakable; now it is death about which we are mute. The unspoken is, nevertheless, both pervasive and damaging. Death seems the most enigmatic phenomenon confronting modern man.

Overarching all man's dreams and undercutting all his accomplishments is the fact that he must die. Whatever he is, whatever he means, man must finally undergo the terrible and debilitating meaninglessness of death. To pretend to understand life without considering death is absurd. Most ridiculous is modern man's enormous effort not to think about death at all.

Judaism confronts death with equipoise and seriousness. It does not permit any euphemism to obscure nor any metaphysics to deny the humanity and, therefore, true mortality of man. The Bible laments the death of Sarah and of Jonathan, of patriarch and king, friend and child. The Jewish funeral service is not without anguish; even in the glorification of God, man weeps over his lost loved ones and his own inevitable death. Even the daily service contains prayers for the dead to remind both mourners and congregation that bereavement and death are a normal, unavoidable part of life.

Judaism takes death seriously, but it does not concede its final-
ity. Only God and the life He offers to share with man are
ultimate. Jewish concern with life after death grows from that
Biblical Sheol where half-living shadows lurk to a full-blown affirmation of the rabbinic dogma of resurrection of the dead. That
development is continuous and organic. Though Bible references
are few, post-Biblical Jewish literature has many descriptions
(Maimonides calls them "riddles" or "figures") of the world-to-
come, which are metaphorical and allusive.

In his early commentary on the Mishnah, the basic law code
compiled in the first two Christian centuries, the Rambam (as
Maimonides is called, from the initials of his Hebrew name)
comments on a passage in the tractate concerning the Sanhedrin
which promises immortal life to nearly all Jews. He analyzes the
nature of the world-to-come in Judaism. Maimonides is of course
opposed to reading the Bible and Talmud literally, in this as
in all other matters. He wants logic as he knows it to prevail, but
he is also opposed to rejecting the Jewish sources out of hand. He
tries to teach us to read them carefully and philosophically. He
attacks both non-believers and literal-minded believers; both
miss the subtleties of Jewish theology.

There is, indeed, a world-to-come, but it is neither physical (as
some rabbinic masters affirm) nor "spiritual" (in the sense of a
body-soul dualism often encountered in present-day thinkers af-
fected by ancient or modern Hellenism). The future life is rather
the full potential of humanity; immortality is being a real man,
with God, and forever. Immortal life is not so much a gift as an
achievement. It is not the miraculous transmutation of man so
much as his continuing perfection. God is our Master, the Torah
our way, and immortality our reward. But God is not simply
like our idea of God, nor the Torah like our over-simplified
literalisms, nor immortality like our wish-fulfillment of never
dying. In this profound analysis, man is complex and mysterious;
the world-to-come is still more mysterious, but at least as real as
we.

What Maimonides stresses is man's capacity to understand, to link himself with the Everlasting. Man cannot be merely an animal with a dog's death. As a physician, the Rambam knows first-hand the human body and its limitations, but as a philosopher he is also impressed by the fuller reality and relevance of mind. Man's participation in eternity is not a wishful thought vainly imposed by a failing body. Eternity is as real as the object of medical science. Both are directly connected with man's mind.

If man can learn to use his mind properly—no easy task, and one to which Maimonides' entire *Guide for the Perplexed* is devoted—then man has a share in eternity. The world-to-come must be won, as Judaism has always taught, and won in this world. The road to eternal life is the affirmation of a link with God which man finds in himself, and which, once cultivated, is his forever. Eternity does not make less of life, but more. Man's responsibility for this world has reverberations that need never die.

FROM

Mishnah Commentary

BY MOSES MAIMONIDES

MISHNAH: All Jews have a share in the world-to-come, as it is said: *Thy people shall be all righteous, they shall inherit the land forever; the branch of My planting, the work of My hands wherein I glory.* But these have no share in the world-to-come: one who says that the resurrection of the dead is not taught in the Torah; one who says that the Torah was not given by God; and the atheist. Rabbi Akiba adds: one who reads apocryphal books or who utters charms over a wound saying: *I will put none of the diseases upon thee which I have put upon the Egyptians, for I am the Lord that healeth thee.* Abba Saul adds: one who pronounces the letters of the Tetragrammaton.

COMMENTARY: I must speak now of great fundamental principles of our faith. The masters of Torah hold differing opinions concerning the good which will come to a person as a result of fulfilling the commandments God commanded us through Moses our Teacher. They also hold widely different opinions concerning the evil which the transgressor must suffer, as a consequence of their different understanding of the problem. So much confusion has invaded their opinions that it is almost impossible to find anyone whose opinion is uncontaminated by error.

One group thinks that everlasting good is the Garden of Eden, a place in which one eats and drinks without any physical work or effort. They also believe that houses there are made of precious stones and beds of silk; rivers flow with wine and fragrant oils, and many other things of that sort. This group believes that the evil *Gehinnom* is a place of raging fire, in which bodies are burned and all sorts of agonies are inflicted upon men. They describe these afflictions at great length. This group adduces proof for their opinions from the words of our sages and from passages in Scripture whose literal meaning seems to agree either wholly or largely with what they say.

A second group asserts that the good for which we hope is the Days of the Messiah, in whose time all men will be angels and all will live forever. Men will be giants in stature and will grow in number and in strength until they occupy forever the entire world. The Messiah will, with the help of God, also live forever. They also believe that in those days the earth will bring forth garments already woven, bread already baked, and many other impossible things. In this view, the worst evil is that a man may not be alive in those days and may not merit the privilege of seeing them. This group also adduces "proof" from many statements found in the writings of our sages and from Biblical verses whose literal meaning seems to agree either wholly or partly with what they say.

A third group holds that the good for which we hope is the resurrection of the dead. By this they mean that man will live again after his death and return to his family and dear ones to eat and drink and never die again. According to this opinion the corresponding evil is that some men may not live after death among those who are resurrected. Here, too, proof is adduced from many sayings that are found in the words of the sages and from Biblical verses whose literal meaning seems to teach this, wholly or in part.

A fourth view holds that the goal of fulfilling the commandments is the achievement of bodily peace and worldly success: fertile lands, extensive possessions, many children, health, peace and security. They also believe that there will someday be a Jewish king who will rule over those who oppressed us. The evil that will overtake us if we deny the Torah is the opposite of these, as we suffer in our present exile. Those who hold this opinion likewise find support for their views in verses of Torah (particularly the curses) and from other passages in Scripture.

A fifth group—and a large one—combines the opinions of all the others. They assert that the ultimate hope is that the Messiah will come, that he personally will resurrect the dead, who will then enter the Garden of Eden where they will eat and drink in perfect health forever.

However, concerning this strange world-to-come, you will rarely find anyone to whom it occurs to think about it seriously or to adopt it as a fundamental doctrine of our faith, or to inquire what it really means, whether in fact the world-to-come is the ultimate good. Nor does one often find persons who distinguish between the ultimate good itself and the means which lead to the ultimate good. What everybody always wants to know, both the masses and the learned, is how the dead will arise. They want to know whether they will be naked or clothed, whether they will rise in the same shrouds with which they were buried, with the same embroidery, style and intricacy of sewing, or in a plain garment which barely covers their bodies. Or they ask, will there still be rich men and poor men, weak men and strong men, when the Messiah comes. . . .

Now I can begin to discuss the matter with which I am really concerned. Know that just as the blind man cannot imagine color, as the deaf person cannot experience sound, and as the eunuch cannot feel sexual pleasure, so bodies cannot attain spiritual delights. Like fish who do not know what fire is because they live in its opposite, the element of water, so are the delights of the spiritual world unknown in our material world. Spiritual delight does not come within our experience at all. We enjoy only bodily pleasures which come to us through our physical senses, such as the pleasures of eating, drinking and sexual intercourse. Other levels of delight are not present to our experience. We neither recognize nor grasp them at first thought. They come to us only after great searching.

It could hardly be otherwise, since we live in a material world and are therefore able to achieve only inferior and discontinuous delights. Spiritual delights are eternal: they last forever, they never break off. Between these two kinds of gratification there is no similarity of any sort. It is, therefore, inappropriate for us who are masters of Torah or theologians to say that the angels, stars, and celestial spheres experience no delight. On the contrary, they really experience great delight in that they know by direct experience the true nature of God the Creator. With this knowledge they enjoy a delight both perpetual and uninterrupted. They have no bodily pleasures, nor could they, since they have no physical senses as we do, through which they could get our kind of gratification.

We will be like them after death! Men who choose to purify themselves will reach this spiritual height. They will neither experience bodily pleasures, nor will they want them. They will resemble a powerful king who would hardly want to go back to playing ball with children as he did before he became king. Such games attracted him when he was a child and was unable to understand the real difference between ball playing and royal power. Like children, we now praise the delights of the body, but do not understand the delights of the soul.

If you consider carefully the nature of these two kinds of delight, you will perceive the inferiority of the first and the superiority of the second, even in this world. Thus, you find that most men exert extraordinary amounts of intellectual and physical energy in order to acquire honor and be regarded highly by their fellowmen. The pleasure which honor brings is not of the same sort as the pleasure derived from eating and drinking. Similarly, many men pursue vengeance over their enemies even more intensely than they pursue any bodily pleasures. Many others deny themselves the keenest of bodily delights because they fear shame and public disgrace or because they seek to acquire a reputation for virtue. If this is the case even in this material world, how much the more must it be so in the spiritual world! That world is the world-to-come.

In the world-to-come, our souls will become wise in knowing God the Creator. This spiritual delight is not reducible into parts, nor can it be described, nor can any analogy explain it. It is as the prophet, awestruck at the lofty magnificence of that good, said: *How great is Thy goodness which Thou has hidden away for them that fear Thee!* Our sages also wrote: "In the world-to-come there is no eating, drinking, washing, anointing or sexual intercourse; but the righteous sit with their crowns on their heads enjoying the radiance of the Divine Presence." In this passage the expression "with their crowns on their heads" signifies the immortality of the soul, that is being in firm possession of the Idea of God, the Creator. The "crown" is precisely the idea which great philosophers have explicated at length. The expression, "they delight in the radiance of the Divine Presence," means that souls will enjoy blissful delight in their attainment of knowledge of the truly essential nature of God the Creator, a delight which is like that experienced by the holy angels who know His existence first-hand.

The ultimate good, the final end, is to achieve this heavenly fellowship, to participate in glory where the soul is forever involved with God the Creator, who is the Cause and Source of its existence.

This is incomparably good, for how could that which is eternal and endless be compared with anything transient and terminable?

That is the meaning of the Biblical statement: *That it may be well with thee, and that thou mayest prolong thy days,* in the world that is infinitely long, add the Rabbis.

Utterly evil punishment consists in the cutting off of the soul so that it perishes and does not live eternally. This is the penalty of *Karet* to which the Torah refers in the phrase: *That soul shall utterly be cut off.* Interpreting this phrase, our sages said: The word *hikkaret* (utterly cut off) refers to the world-to-come. On the other hand, Scripture also says: *The soul of my master shall be bound in the bundle of life with the Lord, thy God.*

It follows that if a person has deliberately and regularly chosen physical pleasure, has despised the truth and loved lies, he will be cut off from that high level of being and remain mere disconnected matter. The prophet has already explained that the world-to-come cannot be apprehended by the bodily senses, in the verse: *The eye hath not seen it, O Lord, except Thou.* The sages taught emphatically that the prophets prophesied only about the earthly days of the Messiah, but that concerning the world-to-come, *The eye hath not seen it, O Lord, only Thou.*

Now let me explain the meaning of the promises of good and the threats of evil punishment which are contained in the Torah. What these promises and punishments mean is that God says to you: "If you do these commandments, I will help you in your effort to do them and to achieve perfection in them. I will remove all the obstacles and difficulties which stand in your way." For it is impossible for a man to perform the commandments when he is sick or hungry or thirsty, or when he lives in a time of war and siege. God, therefore, promises that He will remove all these obstacles to fulfillment so that men who strive to do the commandments will be healthy and safe until they can attain that degree of knowing through which they will merit the life of the world-to-come. However, man must understand that the ultimate reward of doing the commandments of the Torah is not in any of these themselves. And if one violates the commandments of the Torah, punishments ensue. All kinds of hindrances will come into being, so that the transgressor will no longer be able to perform the commandments. It is precisely as Scripture states it: *because thou didst not serve the Lord thy God with joyfulness and with gladness of heart, by reason of the abundance of all things; therefore thou shalt serve thine enemy whom the Lord shall send against thee, in hunger and in thirst and in nakedness, and in want of all things; and he shall put a yoke of iron upon thy neck, until he hath destroyed thee.*

If you consider these things carefully and fully, you will understand that it is as though He were saying to you: "If you do some of these commandments out of love and with genuine effort, I will help you to do all of them, and I will remove the oppressive obstacles that prevent you from doing them. But if you refuse to attempt to perform any of them out of disdain for the commandment, then I will bring upon you the very obstacles that prevent you from doing all of them so that you can never achieve perfect life in the world-to-come." This is the meaning of the statement of the sages: The reward of a commandment is the commandment itself, and the reward of a sin is sin.

The Garden of Eden is a fertile place containing the choicest of the earth's resources, numerous rivers and fruit-bearing trees. God will disclose it to man some day. He will teach us the way to it, and men will be happy there. It is possible that many exceedingly wonderful plants will be found there, plants which are far pleasanter and sweeter than those which we now know. None of this is impossible or improbable. On the contrary, paradise would be possible even if it were not written in the Torah. How much more sure then is it, since the Torah specifically promises it!

Gehinnom is a name for the pain and the punishment which will come upon the wicked. No specific description of this punishment is contained in the Talmud. One teacher says that the sun will come so close to the wicked that it will burn them. He finds proof for this belief in the verse: *For behold, the day cometh, it burneth as a furnace; and all the proud and all that work wickedness shall be stubble; and the day that cometh shall set them ablaze, said the Lord of hosts, that it shall leave them*

neither root nor branch. Others say that a strange heat will be
produced within their own bodies to incinerate them. They find
support for this position in the Scriptural words: *Your own
spirit is a fire which will consume you.*

The resurrection of the dead is one of the cardinal principles
established by Moses our Teacher. A person who does not believe
in this principle has no real religion, certainly not Judaism.
However, resurrection is only for the righteous. This is the
meaning of the rabbinic statement which declares: "The creative
power of rain is for both the righteous and the wicked, but the
resurrection of the dead is only for the righteous." How, after all,
could the wicked come back to life, since they are dead even in
their lifetime? Our sages taught: "The wicked are called dead
even while they are still alive; the righteous are called alive even
when they are dead." All men must die and their bodies de-
compose, of course.

"The Days of the Messiah" refers to a time in which sovereignty will revert to Israel and the Jewish people will return
to the land of Israel. Their king will be a very great one, with
his royal palace in Zion. His name and his reputation will extend
throughout all the nations, even greater than King Solomon's.
All nations will make peace with him, and all countries will
serve him out of respect for his great justice and the miracles
which occur through him. All those who rise against him will be
destroyed and delivered into his hands by God. All the verses of
the Bible testify to his triumph and our triumph with him.
However, except for the fact that sovereignty will revert to Israel,
nothing will be essentially different from what it is now. This is
what the sages taught: The only difference between this world
and the Days of the Messiah is that oppression by other kingdoms
will be abolished. In the Days of the Messiah there will still be
rich and poor, strong and weak. However, in those days it will
be very easy for men to make a living. A minimum of labor will
produce great benefits. This is what the sages meant when they
said: In the future the land of Israel will bring forth ready baked
rolls and fine woolen garments. This is rather like what people

say when someone finds something ready for use. They say, "So-and-so has found his bread already baked and his meal already cooked." The Scriptural support for all of this is the expression, *and aliens shall be your plowmen and your vinedressers.* This verse suggests that there will be sowing and reaping even in the Messianic era. The Talmud records the irritation of one of the sages with a student whose objection to this passage showed that he did not understand because he interpreted the verse literally.

The great benefits which will occur in those days include our release from oppression by other kingdoms which prevents us from fulfilling all the commandments, a widespread increase of wisdom, in accordance with the Scriptural promise: *For the earth shall be full of the knowledge of the Lord, as the waters cover the sea,* and the end of war, again in accordance with the Scriptural statement: *Nation shall not lift up sword against nation, neither shall they learn war any more.* In those days perfection will be widespread, with the result that men will merit the life of the world-to-come.

But the Messiah will die, and his son and grandson will reign in his stead. The prophet has already predicted his death in the verse: *He shall not fail nor be crushed till he hath set the right in the earth.* However, his reign will be a very long one. All human life will be longer, for, when worries and troubles are removed, men live longer. There is no reason for surprise that the Messiah's reign will extend for thousands of years. As our sages have put it: When good is gathered together it cannot speedily be dissipated.

We do not long and hope for the Days of the Messiah because of the increase of productivity and wealth which may occur then, or that we may ride on fine horses and drink wine to the accompaniment of song, as some confused people think. The prophets and the saints looked forward to the Days of the Messiah and yearned for them because then the righteous will finally be gathered together in fellowship, and because goodness and wisdom will at last prevail. They desired it also because of the righteousness and the abundant justice of the Messianic king, because of the salutary influence of his unprecedented wisdom, and because of his nearness to God, as described in Psalms: *The Lord said unto me: "Thou art My son; this day have I begotten thee."* They also anticipate the performance of all of the commandments of the Torah of Moses with neither inertia on the one hand nor compulsion on the other, in fulfillment of the Scriptural promise: *And they shall teach no more every man his neighbor and every man his brother, saying: "Know the Lord; for they shall all know Me, from the least of them to the greatest of them, saith the Lord; for I will forgive their iniquity and their sin will I remember no more."* Similarly, it is written, *I will put my Torah in their inward parts, and I will write it in their heart.* Scripture also says: *And I will take away the stony heart out of your flesh, and I will give you a heart of flesh.* There are many other verses with the same promise.

Then men will achieve the world-to-come. The world-to-come is the ultimate end toward which all our effort ought to be devoted. The sage who firmly grasped the truth and who envisioned the final end, forsaking everything else taught: All Jews have a share in the world-to-come.

Nevertheless, even though this is the end we seek, he who wishes to serve God out of love should not serve Him in order to attain the world-to-come. He should rather believe that wisdom exists, that this wisdom is the Torah; that the Torah was given the prophets by God, that in the Torah He taught us the difference between virtues (which are the commandments), and vices (sins). As a decent man, one must cultivate virtue and avoid sin. In so doing, he will perfect the specifically human which lives in him and will be genuinely different from the animals. When one becomes fully human, he acquires the nature of the complete human being; there is no external power able to deny his soul eternal life. His soul attains that eternal life it has come to know, which is the world-to-come we have described. This is the meaning of the verse: *Be ye not as the horse or as the mule, which have no understanding, whose mouth must be held in with bit and bridle.* Restraints which prevent animals from acting in accordance with their nature are external ones, like the bit and the bridle. With man, the influences which restrain him are his own self-control. When a man achieves human perfection, it restrains him from doing those things called vices which withhold his perfection from him; it urges and impels him toward those things called virtues which bring him to full humanity. This is what all the teachings of the sages have made clear to me about this most important matter.

10

A Man of This World

The hope of Maimonides for immortality sounds easier and more promising than it is. He himself seems to have believed that the indispensable self-realization was both rare and difficult. To learn to be human, which for him implied the painful and hazardous activation of one's intellectual capacity, was man's most important and most uncertain task.

What keeps man from undertaking his redemption under God is mainly his concern for the material things of this world. While Maimonides understood that things might be useful to bribe a child to learn, he had little sympathy for a grown man who preferred owning to knowing. How could it be more desirable to be rich than to be a philosopher?

Moses ibn Ezra, writing in the Golden Age of Spanish Jewry, must have seen more vulgar Jewish acquisitiveness than did the harried Maimonides, who had to flee Spain as a youth, ultimately to settle in Egypt. Ibn Ezra knew many Jews who had fallen in love with "the world," who came to desire fortune and pleasure more than God or His service. His age, so like our own in its affluence, showed him how little man understands his real nature. Ibn Ezra, far more worldly than the philosopher-mystic Bahya, was quite in agreement with him and other religious thinkers that religion requires sacrifice. No man could serve two masters: himself and God. But by serving God he could indeed—Jewish experience said he would—increasingly become that self he ought to be.

The reader may find Ibn Ezra's secular poems rather cynical

in tone, disparaging of what men have come to hold as values and concerns. As a poet, he may be more guilty of exaggeration than the Talmud or Bahya, but he is in agreement with them that man is far from satisfactory. It is because man is unsatisfactory that we need the Torah, the community and the Day of Atonement.

If only man could remember that he must soon die! If only man could see how futile most of his struggle for wealth and happiness seems in the presence of the worm and what the poet calls the "talons of our dust." Death (or heaven) is the only real democracy, in which master and slave, rich and poor are finally at one. Possession cannot deliver from death nor can pride prevail. Man is only a sojourner; his life is wind.

Yet, says Ibn Ezra, God has set eternity in our hearts. The Scripture is true: we are not doomed but called, called to live. For if death and immortality are tragic parentheses around our existence, giving it distance and eternity, it is existence itself that matters most.

FROM

Secular Poems

BY MOSES IBN EZRA

Let Man Remember

Let man remember when alive
That he is prey of death,
So slowly his journey reaches its end
That he thinks he is not moving,
Feels like a man who's safe at sea,
But every day he flies away like wind.

Graves of the Ancient Past

Graves of the most ancient past
Where an eternal folk sleeps eternally.
No hate, no envy among them,
No love or hate of neighbors.
I cannot, when I look at them,
Separate the slaves from the masters.

My Son, If You Should See Me

My son, if you should see me in my grave
A prisoner in chains, living destruction,
Burned in a hole where no one comes or goes,
Like prey in the talons of my dust,
The beauty of my face changed to horror
My flesh clothed in a mantle of worms,
You would not recognize me
So black in color has my face become.

How my relatives have put me off.
My brothers have thought of me as a stranger
My children rejected me—
As I had wilfully rejected my father!

A little while they live on earth.
Their fate tomorrow will be mine.

Go Out to the Court of Death

Go out to the court of death and look
At those who sleep there
Grow shamed, afraid.
See bodies covered with stone,
Dust their cover and their shade.
This is their final resting-place
While there's a world, their dwelling for eternity.

The Man Who Built on Earth

I have seen the man who built mansions
    on earth,
Houses of ivory, and filled them with
    rooms,
And pillars on carved receptacles,
Adorned and richly beautiful,
In a moment turn to heaps
Where none could live,
Ruined palaces.
Say: Where are those who built
    and lived in them
Their souls, their bodies?
What can man hope for except death
The pit before his eyes each day?
Time is a herdsman.
Death like a knife,
And all alive are sheep.

Peace

Peace to those who live in fox-holes
    Dwell in shadows,
Those who were born to the purple
And used to eat delicacies—
They will inherit of all their wealth
Mounds on their back and tombstones.
Fear, earth's children, to look at them!
Be chastened and humbled, children!

A Man Who Sees the Goods of Earth

A man who sees the goods of earth
With wisdom's eyes, finds them despicable.
He puts no hope in gold, nor silver
    trusts. They do not count for him.

His jewels are jokes
He does not turn to gems for joy.
He understands that treasure traps,
Can wipe out his children.
If he should build his nest on stars,
His home upon a bright constellation,
The wind of fate would wreck it there,
Pull down its wood and stones.

Spurn the World

Spurn the world that enriches to
        make poor,
Raises men to eminence to cast them down,
Gives them many children to diminish them,
Gathers their dispersion to disperse,
Gladdens their spirits to bring grief,
Makes their hearts exult to end in fear.
Has there been such a mother who
        bereaved herself,
And permitted no child to escape, survive?

All Who Pass Through the World

All you who pass through the world in power's
        pride,
She hates. She blocks your way.
She brings low whom she raises first,
And disinherits all
Whom she has made rich.
She clothes the heart of strong men with weakness.
Do not covet all her treasuries
Let little be enough to need,
Get provision for the way, death's brother,
So you'll not faint.
The way is much too hard for you.

In Vain the Earth Is Dressed

In vain earth dresses up
Hoping fools will lust for her beauty,
First deceiving them with jewelry
Seducing them with goodly silk,
She ends by hurting them,
Then helping with a very little balm.
She lets them eat a taste of honey-wealth,
Their souls are captive then.
If any man seeks her
Like a garden of delight
He'll find her fruit.

All the Promises of the World

All the promises of the world to us
Are lies; her love of lovers, too.
She gives them wealth to trap them,
Above them hang her nets.
She looks a tree of life
But her tree's fruits are dangerous.
Her words seem to be cool water
But burn her cheeks.

Where walks life
When even days must watch their step?
Where can mankind run
When all its journeys, wanderings,
Are in her hands?

The World Is Like a Foolish Woman

The world is like a foolish woman,
Wind her pomp and glory.
Sweetly she speaks, and yet
Under her tongue is a trap.
Be smarter than her plot, my brother, know

You can turn her power into shame.
Hurry, get rid of her,
Give her a divorce decree!

Children of This World

Men are children of this world,
Yet God set eternity in their hearts
As a law from the day that He created them.

The world is like a flowing brook,
They drink of it and do not have enough.
And would not even
If the sea emptied itself in them.

It is as though its water were salt,
And their thirsty hearts impelled to drink
Like a torrent would it rush into their throats,
But they could never quench their thirst.

Say to the Man Who Trusts in Luck

Say to the man who trusts in luck: Watch out
For her sweet instruction. She lies!
You imagine that she wants to fill your
        heart's desire,
But she doesn't.

And Each Who's Fooled

And each who's fooled by worldly wealth
Believes in the nonsense called bad luck
Or is deceived by his smooth talk
And by the lies his children tell—
Know that if his right hand pours
        out honey
His left gives poison.
What good is money to a truly thoughtful man?

And what does man achieve with
all his work?

The Face of God Alone

The face of God alone I always seek
The secret of my heart I will not tell
to man.
What use is man to man?
What help is the advice of a poor man
To another failure?
Refuse the world that brings her beauty
down
With her own hand, confounds all
true possession.
Two children has she borne.
Within her womb.
One's dead, the other on his back
Is sick to death.

Our joyous acceptance of what is and our efforts to put our lives together in God's pattern are crucial. That is what the Baal Shem Tov taught in his *Testament*, the second document in this chapter. In the very presence of death, he left a message about how to live without despair at failure and without pride at success, how to fear God without being afraid of Him, how to love God without demanding of ourselves more than we can do.

The Baal Shem Tov, Kind Master of the Name, who founded the movement called Hasidism in the Eastern Europe of the eighteenth century, understands man's anguish, perhaps because he lived intimately with all kinds of people. A school-teacher, a friend of carousers and gamblers, a lover of man but no fool, he took Judaism out of the sacred books and gave it back to the people. His message is the overwhelming love of God and the joy that embraces a man of faith even when he suffers. Israel,

Kind Master of God's Holy Name, taught his disciples never to
allow themselves to fall into despair over sin or suffering. For
him, joy was the highest commandment, God the surest fact.

The Baal Shem Tox wrote no books though many have been
written about him. In the *Testament* attributed to him, some of
his insight is directly available. Its extreme brevity should not
obscure its importance; it is one of the great documents of human
piety.

Man, as understood in Judaism and especially in Hasidism, is
what he is only because of God. His suffering is suffering under,
even *with* God. There were many mystical personalities who
were believed to be able to use the Name of God for the benefit
of man. But the Master used the Name in the only really
efficacious way: to make men glad before God. What he was bold
enough to describe as "nonchalance" is the very subtlest kind of
religion. Man must not attach himself to anything or to anyone
in a way that keeps him away from God. But it is God's will
that can link every hour and every person in his life to the
divine. Men are the only sacraments for men. To cling to God,
through men, is beyond our joy or suffering. It is beyond guilt-
feelings and beyond guilt. It is our return to the Source. Man,
surrendering himself, discovers at last who man really is.

FROM

The Testament of Israel,
Master of the Name

I have set God always before me: This verse means that a religious man is calm. I will be nonchalant if I know God is always
before me. It is closeness to God which produces nonchalance.
Trying to get close to God leaves no time to think of lesser

matters. A man who always serves God has no time for pride. If, for example, a sudden fantasy of a desirable woman should come to a man's eyes, or if he should imagine anything gratifying and lovely at all, he must immediately think of the Source of all that beauty in the great power that permeates the world. "If the root of this beauty is divine," he would remind himself: "how can I be attracted to this part only? Is it not better for me to be drawn to the All, the Source of each partial beauty?" If a man tastes something pleasantly sweet he should remember that its good taste comes from the higher sweetness. Reflection like that is reflection on God. If a man hears a funny story and enjoys it, he should think of how his joy itself is part of the world of God's love.

Man must serve God with all his might, for everything has a higher use. God wants us to sense Him in every way. Sometimes a man is taking a walk and talking to other men. He cannot be studying then. But he must still strive to be close to God and to help make God truly One. When a man is hiking and cannot pray as usual, he must find other ways to serve God. He should not agonize over what he cannot do, for God wants his service in every possible form, sometimes in one way, sometimes another. Therefore, when he prepares to travel or to talk with people, he should be prepared to serve God as the situation calls for his service.

He can always be alone with God in his thoughts. He should think only of his love for God and try to grow close to Him. And in his mind he will continually ask: "When shall I be worthy for the Divine Light to live with me?"

Sometimes the Evil Inclination deceives a man into believing that he has committed an enormous sin, when he has only failed to perform a technical part of the law or has done nothing really wrong at all. The Evil Inclination *wants* a man to despair over what he has done so that he feels too guilty to serve God. A person must see through this stratagem and tell the Evil Inclination: "I know you are trying to stop me from serving God by lying to me. Even if I have really sinned a little, God will be happier if I do not make too much of the offense you describe and do not become too guilt-ridden to serve Him. On the contrary, I shall go on serving Him with joy, for it is not my own pleasure I seek but God's. So, even if I have failed, as you tell me I have, God does not want me to agonize over it. The main thing is never to stop serving Him for a moment."

This is the great rule for serving God: as far as possible, do not despair over your guilt.

Crying is very bad, for man should serve in joy. Only if he cries for joy is it very good.

One should not be too anxious about everything he does, for the Evil Inclination uses guilt-feelings to make a man fearful of ever doing anything right. Scrupulosity leads to despair, and despair prevents the service of God. Even if he has stumbled into sin, one must not feel so guilty that he is paralyzed. He should only regret what he has done and turn back in joy to the God who made him.

FURTHER READING

INTRODUCTION

Leo Baeck, *The Essence of Judaism* (Schocken, 1948), especially Chapter 2, "Faith in Man."
Jewish Liberalism's last great book, pre-Auschwitz Europe's last masterpiece of optimism.

Martin Buber, *Between Man and Man* (Macmillan, 1965). *The Knowledge of Man* (Harper, 1965).
Two brilliant books about what man is like, according to psychology and faith.

Nahum Glatzer, *Franz Rosenzweig: His Life and Thought* (Schocken, 1953).
Good summary of one of the most difficult minds of Judaism's twentieth century.

J. B. Soloveitchik, "The Lonely Man of Faith," *Tradition,* Summer, 1965.
Valuable essay by American Orthodox Judaism's greatest teacher.

Chapter 1. *MAN: BATTLEGROUND OF GOOD AND EVIL*

Claude Montefiore and H. Loewe, *A Rabbinic Anthology* (Meridian Paperback, 1960).
Best anthology of Talmudic ideas, with comments by both an orthodox and a liberal scholar.

George F. Moore, *Judaism* (Harvard, 1927–30), especially Chapter 3, "Man, Sin, Atonement."
Classic exposition of Rabbinic theology in English.

Solomon Schechter, *Some Aspects of Rabbinic Theology* (Schocken, 1961), especially Chapters 14–17.
Several brilliant chapters on thinking and teaching of Rabbis.

Arnold J. Wolf, *Rediscovering Judaism* (Quadrangle, 1965), especially Chapter 6.
American Jewish theologians discuss classical problems from different contemporary points of view.

Chapter 2. *MAN: POSSESSOR OF LIFE*

The Code of Jewish Law (Hebrew Publishing Company, 1928), translated by Hyman E. Goldin.
Complete translation of *Kitzur Shulhan Arukh.*
R. J. Z. Werblowsky, *Joseph Karo, Lawyer and Mystic* (Oxford, 1962).
Scholarly biography of author of Judaism's best-known code.

Chapter 3. *MAN: PARTNER OF GOD*

Solomon Freehof, *The Book of Psalms* (Union of American Hebrew Congregations, 1938).
Simply written Jewish commentary.
Johannes Pedersen, *Israel* (Oxford, 1926), especially Chapter 1, "The Soul."
Convincing interpretation of Biblical Judaism's idea of the person.

Chapter 4. *MAN: SERVANT OF GOD*

I. Abrahams, *A Companion to the Daily Prayer Book* (Harmon Press and Bloch, 1966).
Short but scholarly companion to *Siddur.*
Evelyn Garfiel, *The Service of the Heart* (Yoseloff, 1958).
Good introduction to structure of Jewish worship.
Abraham J. Heschel, *Man's Quest for God* (Scribner's, 1966).
A foremost living Jewish thinker tells us what prayer could be.

Chapter 5. *MAN: THE STUDENT*

Solomon ibn Gabirol, *Selected Religious Poems,* translated by
Israel Zangwill (Jewish Publication Society, 1923).
Lovely Victorian translation of medieval poetic master-
pieces.

Chapter 6. *MAN: RESPECTER OF LIMITS*

Bahya ibn Pakuda, *The Duties of Hearts,* translated by Moses
Hyamson (Boys Town, Jerusalem).
The complete philosophical classic in Hebrew and English.

Chapter 7. *MAN: THE PENITENT*

Eliezer Berkovits, "When Man Fails God" in *Great Jewish Ideas,*
edited by Abraham E. Miilgram (B'nai B'rith Book Series,
Volume V, 1964).
Abraham J. Heschel, *Man Is Not Alone* (Harper, 1952), espe-
cially Chapters 20–26.
Judaism as God's idea of man.
H. I. Levine, "The Experience of Repentance," *Tradition,* Fall,
1958.
Fine Orthodox essay on penitence.

Chapter 8. *MAN: THE SUFFERER*

Claude Montefiore, *Outlines of Liberal Judaism* (Macmillan,
OP), especially Chapters 5 and 10.
Classic Reform statement, remarkable for clarity and con-
viction.

Saadya Gaon, *The Book of Doctrines and Beliefs,* translated by
Alexander Altmann (East and West, 1960), especially Chap-
ters 4–9.
Elie Wiesel, *Night* (Hill and Wang, 1960).
Unforgettable biographical fragment.

Chapter 9. *MAN: MORTAL AND IMMORTAL*

Ben Zion Bokser, *The Legacy of Maimonides* (Philosophical
Library, 1950), especially Chapter 5, "Man as a Citizen of the
Universe."
Good introduction to Rambam's mind.
Hayyim Greenberg, *The Inner Eye,* Volume II (Jewish Frontier
Association, 1953), especially "On Death."
Perceptive essay by American Zionism's leading philosopher.
Moses Maimonides, *The Guide of the Perplexed,* translated by
Shlomo Pines (University of Chicago, 1963).
Newest translation of medieval Jewry's greatest philosophical
work.

Chapter 10. *A MAN OF THIS WORLD*

Martin Buber, *Tales of the Hasidim,* Volume I: *The Early
Masters* (Schocken, 1947).
Baal Shem Tov and his followers movingly interpreted for
modern Jews.
Moses ibn Ezra, *Selected Poems,* translated by Emily Solis-Cohen
(Jewish Publication Society, 1934).
Gershom G. Scholem, *Major Trends in Jewish Mysticism*
(Schocken, 1961), especially Lecture 9, "Hasidism."
Penetrating scholarly study of Jewish mystical tradition.

Index